## PRAISE FOR
# *Practicing the Art of Becoming*

"This is a true gem. I love how Patty uses examples from her own life to demonstrate specific steps for knowing and expressing our highest potential. Including ways to approach life's inevitable troubles and challenges as golden opportunities for greater self-loving, freedom, and spiritual awakening." —Phyllis Mitz, M.A. Astrologer

"*Practicing the Art of Becoming* initially caught me off guard - it's not my typical read, but it turned out to be exactly what I needed. Patty's conversational style and relatable examples felt accessible and genuine. I found myself pondering on several of her points while I navigate my own journey of self-discovery. The depth of wisdom in this book leaves me eagerly anticipating her future works - I sense there are many more valuable lessons Patty has to share." —Pranay Gupta, Co-founder, UnlimitMe

"Patty's honesty, openness and innocence are revealing and inspiring. An invaluable asset for anyone seeking to become aware of who they truly are." —Mary Anne Foran, Retired Attorney and Dedicated Student of Becoming

"This is a must read for anyone who has a passion for being an explorer and learning how to take risks in life's continuous journey. Patty beautifully shares her learnings and wisdom, creates enlightenment, and provides guidance with every page. Her lessons in practicing the art of becoming truly are a gift that helps you reach deep into your soul and understand how to reach your full potential." —Lydia Flocchini, Founder and CEO, Scarab Strategies

"*Practicing The Art of Becoming* is pure magic. Reading each of Patty Elvey's exquisite words on the page I felt like I was being enveloped in the golden light of love and unlimited possibility. Through sharing heartfelt and deeply personal experiences, Patty reflects a thorough understanding of how to love and truly own our whole selves, while providing key skills that allow us to move forward, take risks, and overcome adversity by practicing the art of becoming." —Trish Boes, CEO and Founder, UnlimitMe

"Bravely and movingly models the way for us to take the well-worth-it risk to become who we're meant to be." —Kate Hanley, author of *How to Be a Better Person* and host of the "Finding the Throughline" podcast

# Practicing
## THE ART OF
# Becoming

# Practicing
## THE ART OF
# Becoming

Embracing Risk and Discovering
Your Authentic Being

**PATTY ELVEY**

Foreword by California State Senator Josh Becker

Copyright © 2025 by Patty Elvey.

All rights reserved. No part of this book may be reproduced in any form without written permission from the publisher.

Library of Congress Cataloging-in-Publication Data available.
ISBN: 978-1-68555-173-5
Ebook ISBN: 978-1-68555-060-8
Library of Congress Control Number: 2024919288

Manufactured in China.

Editor: Bridget Watson Payne
Illustration: Putra Grafis/shutterstock.com

10 9 8 7 6 5 4 3 2 1

The Collective Book Studio®
Oakland, California
www.thecollectivebook.studio

*With deepest regard for your
Art of Becoming,
I dedicate this book to you.*

# Contents

**Foreword** by California State Senator Josh Becker  9

**INTRODUCTION:** We Are the Sum of All Our Experiences  13

**CHAPTER 1:** Risk and the Art of Becoming  21

**CHAPTER 2:** What Causes People to Lie?  39

**CHAPTER 3:** The Dark Night of the Soul  59

**CHAPTER 4:** Intuition or the Sound of God  73

**CHAPTER 5:** Affirmations: Making It Real  89

**CHAPTER 6:** Forgiveness: Letting Go  103

**CHAPTER 7:** Ask for Help  113

**CHAPTER 8:** Integrity Amplified  125

**CHAPTER 9:** Perception: Take a Second Look  137

**CHAPTER 10:** Listen with Your Heart  143

**CHAPTER 11:** Philanthropy Unlimited  153

**CONCLUSION:** Knowledge, Gratitude, and Destination  165

Acknowledgments  173

About the Author  176

FOREWORD

# California State Senator Josh Becker

Having known Patty Elvey for more than three decades, I can say without a doubt that she has been a trusted source of insight in my life. Whether in business, politics, or personal crossroads, Patty has always had the ability to distill complex situations into their essence, helping me uncover the pathway forward. She doesn't simply offer advice—she empowers you to discover the answers for yourself.

Patty is someone I have always turned to for trust, perspective, and understanding. She brings clarity to complexity, revealing what is true and essential. She has the ability to take life lessons—whether from schooling, formal courses, professional experiences, or everyday moments—and translate them into meaningful guidance. She is not just a comforting presence, but a wise companion. I always leave our conversations feeling more grounded, more confident, and more prepared to take the next step.

Beyond her ability to impact people, Patty has profoundly influenced entire organizations. She was the heartbeat of Lex Machina, shaping our culture and inspiring those around her. Her words and perspective have propelled leaders toward their goals. Her ability to connect with people—whether one-on-one or across large teams—makes her a rare and invaluable mentor. She understands how to navigate difficult decisions with clarity and grace, and those who have worked with her have experienced the profound benefits of her insight and leadership.

With *Practicing the Art of Becoming*, she extends that same guidance to you. It's a practical roadmap for stepping into the life you were meant to live. It will help you

## FOREWORD

identify your path, refine your vision, and make the decisions that align with your true self. Whether you are facing a pivotal moment, searching for clarity, or simply seeking a deeper understanding of your journey, this book will serve as your guidepost.

What makes Patty's approach truly special is that she does not dictate a singular path but rather helps you uncover the right one for yourself. Her ability to ask the right questions and offer illuminating perspectives ensures that the answers you seek come from within. This book captures that essence, providing a framework for self-discovery, growth, and the pursuit of a purpose-driven life.

I know this book will bring that same clarity and inspiration to many more. She has helped me achieve my dreams in my business and political careers, and she can help you achieve yours, too. I am so glad Patty is sharing her experience with the world—this book is a true gift, and I encourage you to embrace the journey it offers.

"To be yourself in a world that is constantly trying to make you something else is the greatest accomplishment."

—RALPH WALDO EMERSON

INTRODUCTION

# We Are the Sum of All Our Experiences

As people around me in high school and college were planning their futures—their careers, their relationships, their families—that was not my focus. I simply could not foresee these things. I could not imagine one plan for my future. I could not relate to the idea of planting roots. My future required taking flight, spreading my wings that had been anxiously awaiting me. I was destined to fly. Though I recognized there could be many landing points awaiting my arrival (and there were!), I wanted that experience of freedom. I already knew that not only was risk a requirement, it would become the wind beneath my wings. I quickly learned flying required great faith, strength, determination, trust, and intention. It was not always the popular choice among my loved ones, but it was mine to make.

Flying provides the opportunity to soar, and soaring offers a viewpoint and a *point of view* that allows me to see the bigger picture. That altitude provides a more complete view of my experiences that in turn enables me to learn their deeper meanings—including greater truths, compassions, understandings, and resolutions.

Soaring also requires a lot of practice. And that—practice, practice, practice—is my constant state of being. Although the elegant, graceful, eagle-esque soaring happens only occasionally, the real purpose of wings is *learning* how to soar. Sometimes, especially in the early decades, I would think I was flying into a beautiful blue sky with wispy white clouds when, in reality, I had lost focus and I was flying directly into the reflection of a tall glass building. *Ouch!* Pain, disappointment, embarrassment, judgment, and confusion would inevitably follow. This analogy now makes me smile—at both my innocence and my enthusiasm when I couldn't tell the difference between the "building" and the "reflection," and at experientially learning the old adage "look before you leap." My wings and I remain in good form, and the journey continues. I've learned so much, including this: the best is yet to come.

We are the sum of all of our experiences. I have heard this, read this, and said this to myself and others. At some point, this statement became my deep truth. And it also became the springboard into my journey of discovering and pursuing *the art of becoming*.

If I am the sum of all of my experiences, it seemed like

it would be a good idea to be interested in receiving *all* the information I could gather—everything that each of these experiences offered. Okay, then, I was interested! And quickly I was all in.

This commitment required me to remove all previous emotional filters and to review (*re*-view) each experience. Good and bad, beautiful and ugly, loving and hateful, happy and sad, graceful and terrifying, blissful and tragic—I unraveled the richness of every seeming dichotomy. Through this process, I could also deeply evaluate, recognize, define, receive, and integrate the benefits and blessings that each experience contributed. This was the *sum of me*.

How did that work for me? It took enormous trust, unequivocal commitment, and unconditional willingness. It was really hard for a long time. Then, it was just arduous. And, as I continue this unraveling, it has become easier.

Difficult as it was, this process has been well worth

the effort. True, it may not be for the faint of heart—it takes great courage to look back with openness and accountability. It requires impeccable honesty, clarity, acceptance, and wholehearted forgiveness. What's more, it requires unconditional love for the process, for myself, and for everyone involved. It requires patience and compassion. And it requires faith and trust that every effort is a worthwhile risk toward the freedom I seek—the freedom that is my heart's desire.

Many years into this journey, I recognized that these steps had become my "stairway to heaven," and I trust the endpoint. I remember the day that analogy first showed up for me. It came at a time when I was exhausted with the process and considered giving up. And then—*boom*—the faith that remained within me, regardless of how I felt, showed me the image of that stairway. I was reinvigorated and rededicated to keep going. The stairway represents to me that I am moving in the direction of freedom and liberation within myself, and with everything and everyone.

In addition to learning from and using the sum of my experiences, along my journey I also listen as others share their own experiences and outcomes. I learn from friends, family, coworkers, and my community—locally and globally—and also through my dreams, meditation, and creative imagination.

Wherever I live or travel becomes my school, an open and unrestricted classroom. It is all here to teach me—and each of us—uniquely. What I extract and achieve while in "class" is entirely up to me, and that can be true for each one of us.

The benefits of learning from my choices increase with each new experience. Each experience deepens my authentic freedom of choice, fueled by responsibility and integrity. Vigilance to this journey became natural and essential. Another adage that honors this vigilance is "He wins who endures to the end!" I choose winning.

Taking risks is key to practicing *the art of becoming,*

therefore; I chose risk as the very first color on the palette I use in creating my art of becoming.

The view, and review, from a greater altitude gave me the perspective where I learned the most: where I became compassionate with myself and others, where I could give and receive equally, and where I experienced grace—even in the face of the most challenging choices and outcomes.

In this book, I share a few life experiences and how I embraced them as opportunities for learning. My attempts to weave their lessons into the tapestry of my being illustrate that I am the sum of all my experiences.

These experiences and lessons may represent a handful of steps on my stairway, or they may represent only one. Either way, I hope you enjoy them, perhaps relate to them, share them, even know just what I mean as I describe them, and maybe recognize your own journey welling up within you as you read them.

"If only LIFE could be
a little more tender and
ART a little more robust."

—ALAN RICKMAN

CHAPTER ONE

# Risk and the Art of Becoming

The word RISK appeared to me one day and began to direct my deep reflection and consideration. I looked back on my life using the present like a magnifying glass, and all I had learned in nearly seven decades became the lens.

I then experienced a directive—or maybe it was more like a challenge—to write. To write a book, based on this reflection, about how the sum of my life experiences had directed my learning. The writing process, with its constant reminders of how deeply personal this journey is, has increased my sense of the value of *all* of it. I am in awe of the lessons. Each one connected to an authentic awareness of my own beingness. And I believe each of us has a unique personal script that directs our awakening to our own divinity—our authentic being. As I've become more aware of my own, I am also more aware of others' divinity, which increases the joy in my life and my experience every day.

When the title of this book first became clear, I believed I knew what it meant to me and why I was writing it. I was able to imagine (i.e., "image in") what could be made possible for others by encouraging them to embrace risk as an entry point into their own discoveries in practicing the art of becoming.

But I was mistaken!

As I began organizing the chapters, I reviewed my own journey. I looked back on my life, and I recognized for the first time that I constantly chose *risk*. Every time I faced a choice, I consistently chose action into the unknown—choosing to follow guidance from a solid, reliable inner source that I knew well but could not name.

Because of the constant movement these choices led to, I had not stopped to reflect or consistently look from a bird's-eye view. But when I did, I could see the greater journey and recognize how each leap had involved risk. I realized there had been acceptance within a life I often resisted, and trust where I often struggled with doubt. Even when I had been focused solely on the present and immediate future, I could now see that I had experienced success by learning from each past situation and carrying those lessons into the next.

I realized this book is not just a reflection on the beauty of risk for others—it's also about my own experience of taking risks, again and again. And it's about challenging the very definition of the word *risk*!

Risk is about the potential for both inner and outer expansion. It is about discovering our strengths, instincts, and so much more—our very capacity for being. I am writing not only about our potential, but also about recognizing the grand opportunity—and, indeed, achieving the probable outcome—of becoming.

Contemplating how deeply I embrace the concept of risk (and how excited about it I am!) led me to reflect on how completely I disagree with the commonly held examples and definitions of the word *risk*.

I googled *risk*, and the first definition that came up was this: "Risk is the potential for harm."

My search results included a list of synonyms of *risk*:

- Threat
- Danger
- Hazard
- Menace
- Peril
- Trouble
- Imminence
- Pitfall

Wow! That sure looks scary. And I challenge it completely!

But here's where it gets interesting: the second line of the definition states that risk ". . . is a prediction of a probable outcome based on evidence from previous experience."

My evidence from consistently choosing the riskier option guided me in each new opportunity and decision. I explore several of the synonyms I claim from my journey in the chapters that follow. The probable outcome—based on my own previous experience—yielded an abundance of practical, usable, valuable knowledge in areas that have shaped my life and values:

- Integrity
- Dedication
- Acceptance
- Trust
- Mastery
- Blessings
- Freedom
- Engagement
- Becoming

As I accepted the challenge and began to write, the words *practicing the art of becoming* became a touchstone for this process. Embracing risk enables us to deepen our authentic experience of being. Another way to say this is, *we practice the art of becoming.* Think of it like the old joke: How does one get to Carnegie Hall? Practice, practice, practice. How does one become the bravest and most liberated version of their divinely created self? By practicing the *art of becoming*!

How has this worked for me? I am a vigilant, committed student. I am a new author. I have a passion for observation, acceptance, awareness, communication, and words. I have memories from very early childhood, and I experience that facet of my own mind as a product of my innate learning nature. I am a student of my own life, and I recognize my journey as one of ardent attempts to make sense of being here on this earth.

As a result of this lifetime of dedicated practice, the practicing itself has become more fun, more natural, and more graceful. Hence my commitment to nonstop practicing. This is what I mean by *practicing the art of becoming*. I am confident there is no end to *becoming*. Rather, it is an ongoing state of discovery we all can live in each and every day. We never need to stop learning and growing. This is my inspiration for not only the most ordinary, but also the most extraordinary, of experiences. And, the best part? We continue becoming, taking away the pressure of finding some finish line, some final score, some winner, some utopia, some nirvana, some heaven. I believe we all just keep on going!

Think again of the saying, *How does one get to Carnegie Hall? Practice, practice, practice.* Even once there, in that coveted location, the practice continues, or one may lose their spot—without constant practice to hone their body of work, one's sharp talent will start to diminish. I believe it is similar with *becoming*. It is impossible to get there; rather, it is an ongoing journey and a unique process of practicing, embracing risk, and discovering one's authentic being.

Personally, I enjoy how often I am gobsmacked, baffled, shocked, amazed, and humbled. While practicing, I am in absolute *awe* of what surprises me: what I did not expect, what I did not see on the path, because the journey is rarely a straight line. Those corners, twists, and turns enrich my experience and expand my possibilities. I truly appreciate a good surprise!

I observe, I witness, I record in an effort to turn

my experience into something usable. How can I learn from this moment, situation, relationship, experience, person, place, thing, or mystery? (This is the *eternally traveling consciousness*—in other words: all things, all the time, in all ways.)

I attempt to use everything in my *becoming*. I note that often the most useful opportunities appear in hindsight, when reflecting on events. This is especially true of experiences that seem to hang on to me, pulling me back to relook, rethink, re-feel, reconsider, reuse, relearn. These are often situations I may have moved on from quickly, not taking the time to extract their lessons. And yet, they might hold the richest learning that lasts the longest. As I have become more practiced, extracting those lessons is easier, quicker, and more natural. This process has become essential for my growth, expansion, and joy.

Another benefit of *becoming* is one I first noticed many years ago. Over forty years ago, I started reflecting on what lay beyond my personal experience and even beyond my wildest imagination. I began to believe that with intention, openness, and practice, the unknowable could simply become the unknown (a possibility), then become known (what is), and finally become ordinarily integrated (usable) into my realm of experience. This mental exercise can be consistently repeated. And, indeed, this is exactly the path of many who move our world forward in many ways—creating great inventions and making great discoveries. Just because you don't know something yet doesn't mean you won't transcend and know it in the future. That is the essence of *becoming*, of using everything; allowing it all to mean something, but not to mean everything; and avoiding narrow-mindedness. That flexibility, that willingness to grow and repeat the cycle of learning, is part of joy. Just keep on going!

When I look further back, I realize that, as a little kid, I did not know judgment, but I did know confusion. I saw and felt a lot of confusion from my very first memory. That observation influenced how I would experience the world—whether in the tiny universe of my home and neighborhood during early childhood or in the ever-expanding landscape of my world as I grew up.

One example was in church where it became evident that there were a lot of rules and expectations. And yet I experienced a lot of confusion. We were learning about commandments. I looked around and didn't see much behavior that matched those directives. Neighbors, family, strangers, nuns, the clergy—all seemed to be ignoring those commandments, even as I was being taught what they meant. I was young, but always observant.

I was taught these commandments in a side room of the church where the young children went while their parents and older siblings were at Mass on Sunday mornings. I was four years old. One of my most fascinating first memories is of the teacher, who, surprisingly, was not a nun—she was a young woman with great kindness in her smile, eyes, and voice and in the heartfelt way she spoke our lessons. I could not help but listen closely to all she had to say and believe every word. I did not experience her as confusing at all. I remember the word *omniscient*. She carefully explained to this group of tiny children that God is everywhere, all the time, all at once, *and always watching me*! She reinforced that "nothing escapes His attention." *That* was the most almighty threat, and I adopted it wholeheartedly. This was an error—one that has influenced me ever since.

In those classes, I absorbed every word and wanted to be the best keeper of God's commandments. For me, these weren't just religious guidelines; they were rules for becoming a good person. I believed that if I kept the commandments, it was clear that I had to be good!

I've struggled with this idea of a rule book for goodness many times in my many decades. Sometimes I embraced the possibility; sometimes I was absolutely at odds with it. Sometimes I was grateful that "someone" cared enough to be looking after me; other times I was deeply resentful at that same "someone." I was often both wholeheartedly grateful *and* wholeheartedly angry. I felt all this and more along the way.

One thing remained consistent: I prayed every day. I had long chats with God, with Source, about everything. I repeated my commitment to follow those rules—so I might be deserving of knowing viscerally and personally the greatest light, loving, sound, care, embrace, acceptance, and protection.

In all of our conversations in my early years, God never hinted, for even a moment, at what was to come—my life, my destiny, my karma, or the trials and tribulations, great and small, that awaited me. The confusion I'd always felt was about to explode exponentially! The good news is, I've survived many explosions—sometimes back to back and at a pace that seemed unbearable. Yet, the most crucial operative words here are, *I survived.*

The beauty of these circumstances was that they created an opportunity for me to take risks—a great many risks. Most often, it was the risk of making a different choice than the one I observed others making. From a very early age, I knew that these choices were not about *them*—I was not acting in opposition to anyone else, or the mainstream—but about *me*. I took the risks to act upon my choices, to do what was right for myself, time and time again. These were not selfish acts; they were actions toward self-preservation. I was making risky choices, on purpose, to become something or someone I could not yet fully see, but in which I deeply believed.

I risked everything, every time, to keep going. I survived every heartache and heart-crushing experience, every extreme emotion and breathtaking fear, and every darkest sadness and complex confusion. I experienced the flow of unexpected—at times unbelievable—moments from likely and unlikely sources, people, and circumstances at both obvious and the least likely places and times.

Through it all, another statement comes to mind, one that goes hand in hand with the ever-important words *keep on going*: "To whom much is given, much is expected."

Even as a newborn, I was gifted with an innate, unconditional knowing that I came from something greater. I have always carried that unwavering sense of connection to what I frequently call God but just as often and easily call Source or simply Greater. That knowledge is my "much is given." It has been, and remains, my medicine, my antidote for all of life's ills. If it were written—like a prescription on a pad or commandments on stone tablets—I believe it would be just one word: *faith*. Faith is the "magic pill," the seemingly mysterious cure for past, present, and future challenges. This is not to say that it is easy, but my experience of living with faith supports my conviction that it is worth the risk to try.

Even as I write this, joy bubbles up and effervesces with sweetness. With my ever-repairing heart, I claim the privilege of remembering and celebrating that I am one to whom much is given. "To whom much is given" is my spiritual promise, and I am grateful.

The "much is expected" part—the burdens and trials we must carry in this life—in fact becomes far less relevant, because that will pass from one day to the next.

Practice continues organically because art is never done—a creative nature always practices toward more creation! I find that every effort, every risk, and every new day and experience are well worth it.

As I practice toward more freedom, I often imagine the creation and learning process as colorful, but with a vibrancy that resonates not only visually but also as sound and vibration—what I envision as "multidimensional" colors. I see my art constantly evolving, and so, too, does the colorful palette that accompanies my journey. This is how my practice has become what I call *the art of becoming*. My palette and the frequencies of color continue to evolve. I'm convinced that practicing moves me toward a beautiful, harmonious masterpiece, even though it remains forever "under construction" while I practice.

I challenge you to consider this: What are you, or are you not, practicing? Is it your *art of becoming*? Just wondering what you may risk? Claiming the artist you are? Claiming what you are *becoming*? Claiming what you may want to become?

I encourage you to reflect on your own practice, your art, your *becoming*, your relationship with risk, your authentic being. Each chapter is just the tip of the iceberg, gleaned from my own journey. I recognize there is often a deeper truth undiscovered, yet practiced. Keep on going!

"You have power over your mind—not outside events. Realize this, and you will find strength."

—MARCUS AURELIUS

CHAPTER TWO

# What Causes People to Lie?

I believed it was inconsiderate and cowardly to lie. I saw the effect lies had as I observed friends, family, and even strangers impacted by deceptions, misleading promises, absolute falsehoods. Of course, that lead me to wonder what causes people to lie, myself included. Sometimes it is "on purpose," an intentional choice, and in those cases, it's most often for the liar's own reasons. But other times it happens so quickly that the words are spoken almost before any thought can be given to them, seemingly before any choice is made. In these latter cases, lying may be unplanned, unintentional, involuntary, or accidental. What matters is, once it's done, what comes next?

If we've lied and regret it, what are our choices for corrective action? Words spoken can never truly be taken back. Such words may not be forgotten—either by the speaker or the recipient—as much as we might wish they would be. The best-case scenario is that admitting a lie creates a complex scenario, the beginning of an entire journey of unraveling the lie, steeped in honesty and forthcoming truth—with hefty heartfelt sides of compassion and forgiveness. I have never experienced a lie being "undone," but I have chosen resolution and healing. Without resolution, the effects of a lie can be long-lasting: emotionally crippling and even sabotaging what is to come.

I clearly remember the first time I made a conscious decision to lie. It was a compelling choice at the time and, upon reflection, taught me a lot. As a young child, I loved the lessons of the commandments, and I believed, as I was taught in Sunday school, that if you lived by those directives, you were good. I wanted to be good for sure, and "thou shalt not lie" meant lying was not an option. I grew up in a smallish town and, when I was eight years old, because of my asthma, our local doctor referred my parents to take me to a specialist in the big city, almost three hundred miles away. Driving to my appointments created challenges and tension in our home every time. Most often, my mother would drive me, but on this particular day, it was decided my father would be the one. These were always long days, with the long drives both ways and usually a few hours at the doctor's office in between.

My father never talked to me much (that's another chapter—or maybe a whole book!). This day was no different, even though we would be together from dawn to dusk. When we started out, it was not long before I realized something was unusual. He did not take the road to the turnpike that Mom always took, or that we had taken together when both he and Mom had brought me for my early diagnostic appointment. This day, we were driving through the mountains, and when I asked him why, he said he was taking the back roads because it was faster.

Then he made a stop. He told me he had to make a special work delivery. The stop was at a small storefront in an old, rickety-looking home—there were many such places along those back roads "up the mountain," as we called it. There was a sign for a small convenience store just inside the door of the house where local folks would buy their bread, milk, a few other daily staples, and snacks. My father drove a delivery truck for our town's bread company, and his regular delivery route included this rural area. He got out and firmly told me to stay in the car, adding, "Be good," or something along those lines. I was excellent at listening to firm directions and planned to barely move a muscle. He got a few loaves of bread out of the trunk of the car and walked up to the open door where, from the car, I could see through the screen there was someone inside.

I was sitting at the window in the back seat of the car behind the driver's seat. It seemed like a long time went by, more than enough to complete the special delivery of a few loaves of bread. When I looked out the window—without moving a muscle, as planned—I saw my father standing with a woman in the curtainless second-floor window of the house. That was unexpected. There was a dashboard clock in our 1960 Ford Fairlaine, and I watched it tick away forty-five minutes. I was quiet and sat still the entire time. I was good, even though I wondered if we would be late to my doctor's appointment. Then my father returned. He got in the car, and a woman walked through the screen door and stood on the porch in a long pink bathrobe. She had long dark hair. She stood, her head tilted to one side, smiling and waving until we pulled away. I was sitting behind my father and saw that he had wet hair, so much so that it was dripping on his shirt collar. I asked him why, and he said he was just so tired he had to splash water on his face and may have used too much. I knew he was lying, and it had looked like the woman in the pink robe had wet hair, too.

That day, I knew I would have to lie to my mother when I got home and she asked about the trip. I felt it in my heart, in my stomach, in my throat, and even in my eyes, which stung as I held back my confusion and hurt. I also could not let him know how much it hurt or that I understood I could not tell my mom the truth. What I understood was that I was witness to a breach of loving. I assure you; I did not understand what happened between them physically inside that house, but my heart was aware that this was not something my mom would welcome hearing when I told her about my trip to the doctor with my dad.

And there I was: lies all around. I could practically see the lies flying all over the place—around my father, that woman, anyone else who lived in that house, myself, and anyone I had to tell an abbreviated story to about the day because it was not the whole truth.

The nuns used to say that lies were black spots on your soul (yes, *high drama*). Regardless of the soul part, it felt clear to me that the black lies were all around that house and in the car, and now I had my very own lies. Was it possible that I could still be good?

I was sick with the emotional circumstances. I was angry with my dad and the woman who seemed to think it was okay to involve me—as if I did not matter, as if I were ignorant, or worse, as if they thought of me as just some stupid, irrelevant kid. It was not fair; it was selfish of them; it was confusing to me; it was bad; it was wrong; it was ugly. I became a part of it, unwillingly but completely, because I had to proceed with guarding the lie somehow. I already knew my mom had felt betrayal in the past, because of things my father had said and done before that day. But I had known that because of observation and the empathetic connection I had with her. I was not emotionally prepared to feel these things personally, directly, and as my own, at the age of eight. The agony was overwhelming.

Trust me, I learned a lot about the difference between ignorance and innocence that day! I also learned more about the way I process information. My strategy of keeping things inside greatly increased that day, and it would become a lifelong practice. I misguidedly thought this repression was the pathway to self-preservation—mostly because I did not know of any safe place to freely share what I knew without consequences. I became silent. It was the closest I could come to honesty, given what I was seeing, hearing, and knowing. In my journey of learning through reflection, I now recognize how, in most situations—basically, all the time—I understood so much for my age.

I was born with tremendous curiosity, astute observation, a clear memory, and a profound desire to understand people and their behavior. My overarching desire was simply that I wanted everything to make sense! (Ha ha—*as if that could ever happen!*) Living with my six siblings and my parents, there was a lot going on around me all the time for me to observe and try to make sense of. But as my world expanded—and continues to expand even today—I moved toward allowing things to *make sense "as is."* This gentler approach allowed me to fulfill the heartfelt desire for understanding that I adopted as a wide-eyed little girl. Even though that quest began in the most authentic innocence and heartfelt ignorance, it was driven by a curious little human, brand new to the world and with so much happening all around her.

It took me a long time to unravel this predicament about lies. The first step was recognizing I was not at peace about it. And if I thought I was, that was simply untrue. And if it was untrue, then I had to admit I was actually lying to myself. In that admission, I began to become more honest, more courageous, and stronger in new ways. I hesitated over and over again. I did not like the realization that I was perpetuating a lie. Looking ahead, I didn't like knowing I couldn't experience the peace I believed in until I unraveled this!

The risk before me was in committing to the truth. In doing so, I had to admit that I was lying to myself about a lot of things. Most of my lies to myself were my own illusions on both ends of the inner/outer spectrum—with trust and trusting on the inward-facing end of the spectrum, and safety and security on the outward-facing end.

In my later years, when I decided to risk unraveling the lies I had kept deeply buried, it became necessary to take bigger and bigger risks. I uncovered memories from my lifelong practice of keeping things inside, ranging from when I was very young (I have very early memories because my mom was struggling at the time) through my next six decades. I uncovered sad things, happy things, tragic things, heartbreaking things, exciting things, adventures, and disappointments—along with surprising lies, as well as some enthusiastic truths.

There was no clear pattern to what I found, but I do know that in the processes of seeking peace—of uncovering memories and getting honest with myself about where I had lied to myself, both about my experiences and my level of peace with them—I can honestly say that I took a great risk: the risk of facing the truth. My present-day lens of higher altitude and greater perspective illuminated this truth, making it easier to see and, therefore, more fluid to process it.

Upon reflection, I recognize that this was a critical aspect of my practicing the *art of becoming*. I am seeing the benefits of practice, practice, practice. My first benefit is that I am much better at living in the moment, in the present. Second benefit is that I am engaging with the peace that is available in each moment because I've chosen to let things *make sense "as is."* And lastly, I am willing to prioritize practicing the review from higher altitude, which enables me to reveal deeper meanings, and sometimes discover deeper lessons.

The greatest outcome of practicing this behavior is essential to my freedom—the primary quality that drives me to keep going. In my utmost honesty and heartfelt truth, I see, hear, and feel that it is vulnerability that also guides my ability to accept the *"as is."* For this color, I am adding gold to my palette.

When I looked back at my first intentional lie and its circumstances from a higher altitude, with more illumination and honesty—and after years of practicing the *art of becoming* and employing the principle of allowing everything to *make sense "as is"*—I was finally able to remove judgments, expectations, and concepts such as right and wrong, good and bad, and sins of the soul. Instead, I could see that there was so much emotional currency involved on that day I rode with my dad—both for myself and everyone present! I felt sadness for my father, for the woman, and for whatever their motivations were. I know it had nothing to do with me. Odd as it may seem, I can still see the house, the woman, the back of my father's head as he drove, and the clock on the dashboard, but I do not remember talking to my mom or even seeing her when we got home from our trip. My decision not to tell my mother was already buried deeply inside me by the time we returned home. I never challenged my dad on his explanation (or lack thereof). My lie became a combined version of truth, withholding, and fantasy when I later spoke of how the day was for me.

I managed to process the day somehow, and in my patterns of behavior, I learned how to file away those things I couldn't figure out or didn't know how to deal with at the time. I practiced that for a long time. And I assure you, what I was *becoming* by employing that behavior and those options was nothing like who or how I truly wanted to be!

So, why do people lie? What made me lie? My experience revealed the most common purpose of lying may be, in some way, to "save" ourselves. Self-preservation is protecting ourselves from consequences, even if only perceived consequences. In my observations of others and my own close-up experiences, I noticed the choice to lie seems to override any remorse, at least in the moment, for fear of those consequences.

But is lying acceptable when it feels like the best choice among bad options? Or when it may provide more comfort, or less heartache, to replace the truth with a lie?

These are always interesting ethical questions when they arise, and they closely relate to my painful and difficult choice to lie to my mother.

Although lying is often an option—when all possibilities are carefully thought through and well-reasoned—personally, I prefer to resist the lie in all circumstances. Rather than lie, I've found it useful to use silence as a placeholder and await a better opportunity to discuss the truth. For me, any lie is a last resort. That old adage about how the truth will always come out? Well, I think that is accurate.

In my observation, it appears as if sometimes lies

are intentional, on purpose, and outright. I have experienced this behavior and often recognized a sense of self-preservation in the one telling the lies (much like my choice when I decided to tell my first lie to my mother). Even if such lies are not meant to harm others, there is often collateral damage. For many years, when I encountered a "liar," I wanted to understand them more deeply and offer my *help* in some way. I thought if I could recommend an alternative—another, more honest option for self-preservation—I might change their behavior. My introduction of a revised approach has never had any effect on the liar, but it did wear me down and completely exhaust me emotionally!

As I continued my journey of discovering and understanding my own behavior, I discovered that thinking I could *help* was a lie of my own, not to mention an overreach of responsibility. Although it was not a lie I was telling outright, it was one I was living through my actions. Much to my surprise, I realized the only outcome of this behavior was that it was compromising my own freedom!

Such revelations continue to amaze me. I was truly unaware of the personal cost of directing my energy, attention, wishes, and "help" in this manner. The misdirection of my heartfelt intention was comparable to being chained to an unmovable post; there was only so far I could move because of the chain, limited as I was by things that weren't "mine." In clearer and more honest words: I was limiting myself and avoiding focusing on myself. I was seeing myself through the distorted reflections of lies that liars directed toward me.

The day I took a long, hard look at myself was a peak "aha" moment. Gaining perspective, using reflection and altitude, I saw my behavior of over-responsibility. And I admitted that pattern can be futile. Now I had to be ruthlessly honest with myself about my behavior and my relationships with people around me.

I have self-compassion in this case, which is somewhere between accepting and condemning my taking over-responsibility. In some circumstances, I accept my behavior—hence the compassion. However, I ultimately prefer to stay outside the sphere of over-responsibility as much as possible.

Once again, I emphasize the value of using everything for learning, growth, expansion, upliftment, insight, acceptance, and understanding. This commitment to *usability* provides a safer approach for choosing the most authentic honesty. The desire for self-preservation, or even over-responsibility, becomes an opportunity for *usability*. With the intention to *use everything*, the risky choice—to take action, both inwardly and outwardly, operating from the truth and embracing the consequences of that choice—is actually kinder, gentler, and even easier. It is the golden choice.

I noted earlier that my magical antidote for life is faith. My magical antidote for honesty is forgiveness.

Forgiveness, in turn, breeds peace, which allows for freedom to become our authentic selves. These prescriptions are exceptionally effective for relationships—both with ourselves and with others.

If we are willing to risk our self-determined positions of right and wrong, us and them, and instead become the best of our intrinsic human nature, we move toward harmony, something I believe we are designed for. If we really are meant to get along, the simplest solution may be to start with any two humans relating honestly to one another. This is a demonstration of practicing the art of becoming and discovering our authentic being in relationship.

"You have the right to wonderful things. You just have to believe and feel it. Go ahead and Bless yourself."

—POPE FRANCIS

CHAPTER THREE

# The Dark Night of the Soul

I was surprised not only to receive a call from my friend after many years, but also by the invitation she extended and her request for my help.

We had been good—maybe best—friends, in our mid-teens, before either of us had a driver's license or a car. I probably spent as much time with her as anyone in my peer group. We would sit outside on our porches; sometimes we picked blueberries and baked pies, or we walked to the community pool in the summer. We talked about more things than I did with anyone else at that time. She moved away in high school and we'd connected only a few times in the years before she called.

The reason for her call, so many years later, was that she was in psychotherapy, and her therapist had encouraged her to reach out to me. She wanted to meet in person so I could help support and validate her memories from our teenage years.

I was hesitant at first—it was a long drive to an unfamiliar area—but I agreed and, honestly, found I was looking forward to catching up.

I never imagined what would follow.

We agreed to meet for a weekend in the Poconos in Pennsylvania—halfway between our two homes. It was autumn, a beautiful time of year in the mountains, and the trip would be a nice break from the cities where each of us lived.

I realized it would be great to see her. She had been one of the most beautiful and mature girls in our school. She seemed confident. She read a lot, which gave her a deeper understanding and more verbal expression than I had at the time. She was brilliant and often made bold choices. The truth is, her own life circumstances presented an ever-changing environment, and sharing with me about that spurred our childhood bond.

I, on the other hand, was much quieter and more timid. I preferred to find and blend into the silence, finding invisibility to be my most comfortable way to show up—not only in the years we were friends, but for decades beyond as well. I was not confident and certainly didn't take as many risks in those days.

Looking back, it *was* a risk to say yes to this invitation. And, as I discovered in the days that followed, it was the first of many risks that would change the trajectory of my life.

I arrived in the Poconos and was cheerfully greeted by my friend. The fall weather was chilly, but the cabin was warm and cozy. I learned that her marriage had ended, and the story she told was both surprising and heartbreaking. I remembered a comment she'd made about her husband in one of our few conversations between the ages of 14 and 40; she had said that meeting him was like "finding a diamond in a coal mine." That image had spoken volumes, and I'd been happy and excited to hear the love and enthusiasm in her voice. Hearing the story now of their marriage's dissolution was heartbreaking.

We talked for hours and stayed up later than planned. I think there was wine with the dinner she prepared. The next day, we took a long walk surrounded by the beautiful autumn sunshine and colors, still talking and talking. That evening, we went to a local bar for dinner and had a few beers as our conversations continued. Over all those hours, we shared memories of our families and time together as teenagers, along with minor updates about our present lives.

On Sunday morning, before packing our cars, we sat for a while and discussed the value and success of the weekend in supporting her therapy goals. She felt that the sweetness of sharing our memories gave her the validation she was seeking. We were confident her therapist would be happy with her progress and the outcome of our time together.

Then, somehow, she shifted the focus of the conversation to me. I was surprised—maybe even shocked—because all my communication skills, my usual way of interacting with others, centered on keeping attention on *them*—and, by default, off *me*. But she really turned the tables, and instead of a mutual sharing conversation, she was suddenly running down a list of memories in stark contrast to what she believed I had portrayed in our conversations all weekend.

In a short time, she voiced her experiences, observations, and familiarity with the rhythms of my own life and the expectations weighing on me during those formative years. She wasn't merely invalidating the (now so-called) memories I shared, she was denying them and questioning my (now so-called) ability to remember. What's more, she filled in "truths" as she remembered them from having been near my family, inside my home, and around my responsibilities. I would say it was mind-boggling, but in truth, it was absolutely *memory*-boggling!

I had never given myself the opportunity to reflect and to consider my memories in this way. And I was certainly not prepared to begin at that moment.

I barely remember driving home. I was not okay. It felt as if the pin had been pulled from an emotional grenade, and I knew an explosion was inevitable. What was I going to do about it? How could I handle it? *Would* I handle it, or . . . ?

I sat up all night. The ticking of the grenade continued. I prayed for any signs, guidance, *help*. By Monday morning, I still needed more time. I couldn't move, let alone move forward. And yet, I knew without a doubt that an outcome lay ahead. I had to do something. No matter what direction I took, any action on my part would be a gigantic, never-before-experienced risk.

I was always very reliable at work—never sick or even late. But that Monday morning, I called my employer before business hours and simply said I wouldn't be coming in. He must have picked up on the ticking time bomb in my voice, because he asked, "Will you be okay?" I was surprised, and the only answer I could give was, "I hope so." He asked when I would be back, and I said, "I don't know." That was it. I closed the blinds in my bedroom, and for four days I stayed there—crying, sobbing, screaming, and fighting with the invisible memories.

I had never cried like that before, although I remember times when I wanted to but held back, held in, held on. My brother had died suddenly in a car accident several years earlier, and my weeping at his funeral opened onto a sadness I could never face again. And yet, there was so much more in the depths I was feeling and always denying. I was terrified to feel everything I'd suppressed over the years—things I'd made excuses for, things I'd accepted misplaced responsibility for, all the things I saw, heard, thought, refused to believe, and more.

I was always afraid that if I let myself feel any of it, I'd also feel an uncontrollable, underlying anger. And if I felt that anger, I could never forgive myself. I'd watched anger destroy love, relationships, and families over and over again. I never wanted to contribute to such destruction. So my entire life, I tried to navigate around anger. I avoided accepting that I felt it at all—and that I knew it intimately and honestly. I denied all of it. How did I not see this wasn't working?

Well, I found out when my friend, in a simple moment

of honesty and friendship, unknowingly opened my Pandora's box in that cabin in the Poconos.

For those four days of sitting, lying, and fighting in my dark room, I prayed—for help, for direction, for choices, so I could figure out what to do next. I had to be honest with myself, and I recognized I couldn't go on as I had before. So, if there was no going back, what would moving forward look like, feel like, be like? And how would I get there?

I prayed to be shown the way. And I wholly understood that among my options, not moving forward at all was one of them. What I didn't know was this wasn't even the scariest choice!

At one point in the dark, in the middle of the night, my ability to hang on in the unknowing faltered. At the same moment, my deepest prayer for *help* crashed into my room, and the direction I had cried out for was suddenly before me. My room was no longer dark, and I was confronted with my *other* option.

I experienced—saw, felt, heard, and *recognized*—the anger I had long denied. It was there with me, standing on the bed, dark, angry, animated, and terrifying. The silence became so very, very loud, and this fire-breathing dragon was going to make me choose.

I was paralyzed for a moment before I remembered that this was the help I had prayed for. I needed to figure out what to do with it. What did it mean? And—*oh no*—I heard the answer to my prayer loud and clear and I wasn't sure if I could respond. *Help* was telling me I *had* to embrace this anger. It was a part of me, a part of the whole, and I couldn't deny it any longer. To do so would be to deny that I could control my choices around anger. I could choose to stop being held hostage, to stop being limited.

I *had* to embrace this. I reached out and hugged the terrifying, fire-breathing dragon. As I did, I noticed my heart was quiet and my breathing was soft for the first time since I'd been in that cabin with my friend.

It was daylight and a small ray of sun peeked through the blinds. I was okay, just as I had hoped I would be.

In this state of "okay," I felt relief, I felt alive, I felt free, I felt courageous, I felt capable. And I knew clearly that it was no longer necessary to deny what I was feeling. Embracing the terror "grew me up," so to speak. I did not have to be afraid of becoming what I feared. I was strong. I had conquered the dragon I had created, nourished, and cared for all those years. Somehow, I had believed this dragon was a protector, but in that dark night of the soul—*my* soul—the truth was revealed. The dragon was, in fact, my separation from my truth, from my strength, and from the innate wisdom of my soul, prayers, and dreams. For the first time, I was free to be whole and to practice my *art of becoming*.

Also, the ticking stopped and has never returned. The time bomb dissolved. I will never forget the amazing combination of emotions that converged in the moment I chose to embrace the dragon in that dark night. Even now, more than thirty years later, tears gently flow as I write this, because the memory remains so powerful. That one moment was a culmination of ultimate terror, necessary surrender, and blind faith.

When I reached forward and hugged that dragon, I hugged myself—because that dragon was a part of me: all the anger I had denied, all my worst nightmares, and all my deepest fears, all my most painful, unspoken heartaches. It was truly life or death for me, even if not physically. If that darkness in the night had gone any other way, it would have meant giving up my soulful, seeking, truthful nature—the death of the woman I am now.

I faced the pinnacle capstone of my dark night: recognizing the dragon and acknowledging my darkest fears also required courageously embracing the dragon and those fears to claim the freedom I craved. The transformation from darkness revealed the LIGHT. By no longer fearing those dark emotions, I was freed from their control. I quickly discovered choosing LIGHT also was choosing life, my life, my freedom.

I now do that every day. It's divine to know and remember the light is always there. I add the color of radiant LIGHT to my palette as I practice the *art of becoming*. It shines brightly.

In all my risky choices, I recognize that the greater risk is forgetting this way of being. A great way to resolve any gaps—and the antidote when in those gaps—is to say outwardly or inwardly, *I forgive myself for forgetting that I am divine!*

"When you talk, you are only repeating what you already know. But if you listen, you may learn something new."

—DALAI LAMA

CHAPTER FOUR

# Intuition or the Sound of God

My art and practice of becoming includes deepening, embracing, enriching, and sharing from a sacred place inside of me—a place that includes aspects that may be mental, emotional, heartfelt, soulful, inspirational, imaginal, or a combination of these. I recognize this sacred place by the unencumbered peace and freedom I experience when I share from it. I call this place my *beingness*. I also know when I'm not in that place. This *beingness* is unique to me and exists in a constant flow, updating with every action, thought, and deed. You, too, have a unique *beingness*, and as you *listen*, you may discover more about your own sacred place within.

*Beingness* is never stagnant—it can't be. Who I was even an hour ago is past, yet my *perception* of the past is a tool that fuels and accelerates *becoming* in the present.

Using the viewpoints of the present while looking back into my history offers higher perspective. These viewpoints include *altitude* (looking down from above for a broader, more inclusive perspective on the landscape); *illumination* (gaining clearer vision by focusing a greater light on a situation); and *maturity* (maturing up, applying insights from new experiences to past events and relating to my history with an evolved point of view). Each of these higher-perspective viewpoints brings more honesty, more authenticity, more openness. With these, I engage with my life, with others, and with the world around me with more interest and involvement.

One strategy of maturing up is *listening*. I continue to make listening a priority on my path of learning, growth, and expansion—leading me toward the peace and freedom I was always seeking and still seek. This peace and freedom are unwavering, nonnegotiable aspects of my *becoming*. So far, I've found that there's always more freedom to seek.

I'll take a risk at this moment and divulge honestly: the practice of listening has been, and can still be, *hard*! My mind isn't always focused, present, kind, sensible, understanding, receptive, or mature. When I first began exploring this journey, this *art of becoming*, my mind seemed to have no concept that patience was even an option—instead it just raced toward failure of freedom time and time again.

Genuine, authentic, heartfelt listening requires patience! I began by listening to myself first. It wasn't an instant change in my attention, focus, or behavior. It required constant practice and commitment. Experiencing a few moments of peace encouraged me to keep going, and as I found more and more peace, I developed further. As you move forward with your own listening practice, it may help you to remember these three *P*'s: patience, practice, and peace.

Applying a similar practice to *receiving* delivers greater receptivity when listening. In other words, listening requires truly hearing—or receiving the message. I discuss listening with your heart later in this book, but here's a hint: Did you ever notice that *hear* is within the word *heart*?

Listening reveals an imperative question: *Who am I listening to?* Answering that question was one of my first significant risk investments on my journey. And it remains a standout. The rewards from making conscious choices about whom to listen to have been transformative, and result in my experience of greater peace.

Before I understood the essential importance of asking *Who am I listening to?* I had already wandered far into the dangerous, treacherous, and injury-ridden minefields of listening to *other people's opinions*. I didn't realize I had the option to discount, debate, or ignore those opinions. And I certainly didn't perceive the vast distance between others' opinions of me and what was actually true and authentic about me. I listened and believed others knew better and knew me better. As a result, parts of me were often paralyzed or blown apart, creating downright agonizing pain. In my defense, ever since I was young, my feelings were primarily rooted in fear and survival—and those feelings continued for much longer than I am happy to admit. They contributed to my lack of self-confidence and left me vulnerable to believing others knew better.

Thank goodness those bumps, bruises, broken hearts, seemingly catastrophic injuries, and my sense of devastating carnage were often not physical. When I recognized I had a new choice about whom to listen to, I was able to recover my sense of self—with attention, intention, strength, support, learning, commitment, extraordinary effort, and a heavy-duty prescription of faith. That faith became the gateway on my path of *becoming*. Once I saw it was illuminated, I was able to move toward it with eyes wide open.

*Who am I listening to?* Also included: *What parts of myself am I listening to?* The child forced to grow up too soon, the hurt teenager, the angry daughter, the disappointed fatherless girl, the impatient young woman, the confused student, the scared girlfriend, and so many other voices. Sometimes a new one showed up, but much of the time the conversations, monologues, and dialogues with those parts of myself were on repeat.

It was very much the same with other people's opinions, which became more frustrating and challenging as they looped on repeat. I had wanted to change others' opinions of me into something good—I had hoped to influence their point of view. But I realized I could no longer believe only what they said; to do so would extinguish what *me* remained—even though that *me* was coiled so tightly inside me.

Ruthlessly integrating, *'Who am I listening to?'* into my routine behavior was the risk that launched my journey of *becoming*. And *wow*, practice became an absolute necessity!

My path is one of seeking a way to make sense—or even just "more sense"—of being human. Along the way, I explored options that I thought might deepen my understanding, some riskier than others: I revisited the Catholic church, where I had roots from a very young age; I fell to peer pressure and briefly explored drugs that are now legal in many states in the U.S.; and in a riskier endeavor, I followed a guru who promised "knowledge" through meditation (I even traveled alone to Miami Beach for Guru Puja—*very* risky at the time). Each of these experiences became lessons in my personal classroom of observation and witnessing.

Then an opportunity arose that, though it seemed safe enough on the surface, was at the time the riskiest for me of all. Someone I met at work invited me to an event on personal accountability, responsibility, and taking charge of your life. My first reaction was, "Not interested." But, in truth, the invitation shook me inside, leaving me with a blend of fear and excitement that caught my attention. Because of that feeling, I decided to attend. That event was the entry point to choosing myself, to truly taking charge of my life and my well-being. It is a choice I continue making every day.

As I began to take charge of my life, one of the first things that became clear was that I could honor my sense of *knowing* that had always been with me and began at my earliest memory. I wondered if this knowing was intuition or something else.

The *Oxford English Dictionary* defines *intuition* as "the ability to understand something immediately, without the need for conscious reasoning." That surely matches aspects of my experience from a very young age.

Intuition is often referred to as a "gut feeling"—authentic, powerful, directional, useful. It is often acknowledged as a generational or inherited trait. I was told that I come from a long line of intuitive women on my mother's side. And, although I spent much less time with my father, I have come to believe he also carried this intuitive trait. Upon reflection, I see evidence of his deep intuitive knowing in the love he pursued with my mother.

Growing up, I was consistently surprised with how much I seemed to know about the world despite limited life experience. We did not venture far from our small personal world—house, school, church—and even our TV was limited to just two channels in my youth. I identified as an observer and began to recognize that a lot of information was coming forward in my awareness *about* what I observed. And that information was not coming from other people telling me directly or from overheard conversations.

This information was always useful, even practical,

and comforting when I felt unsure or afraid. It made sense. Long before I could even read, I understood that it was coming from a deeper or a higher source. Though it wasn't physical (no writing on the wall, etc.), the information would simply come to me, heralded by a *feeling* that would capture my attention, urging me to listen and be ready to receive. Over time, I learned to recognize this feeling was a signal for the accompanying communication that I began to refer to as the *sound of God*. If other language resonates more with you, it could also be called the *sound of the Source*, the *sound of the Universe*, and the *sound of the All*.

This sound has never been thunderous, scary, or overbearing. I experience it clearly and quietly. The quiet delivery of the communication contributed to my comfort when I was young. And the feeling that accompanied it was a sacred essence.

It would be many years before I asked questions and answers followed. I continue to ask on occasion, and when I'm patient, answers are clear and directional.

However, I don't believe the questions are necessary. Rather, I devote my time and energy to listening and the benefits that follow.

Though separate from my experience of the *sound of God*, I also acknowledge and appreciate my intuition. It's active and useful and I reliably engage with it in daily interactions with people and places. My intention is to trust that I will get the messages meant for me, and the more I listen, receive, and act on those messages, the more they flow.

Although there were times when I doubted, rejected, or discarded what I was hearing, I noticed that I continued listening and evaluating the support these messages provided regardless. Eventually, I began actively communicating by asking questions. Both intuition and the *sound of God* are two-way communications—even if I'm not asking questions, listening is still an active role on my part, and my participation keeps this communication open and flowing.

If this sounds familiar, that's because it's very much the same with personal communication in the physical world. Interpersonal communication is an art that operates in approximately eight billion different ways—one for each human being! There's still time for us, the human population, to discover, or uncover, the secrets to communication.

Until then, let's have fun—doing our best to listen to ourselves first so we can share with others from a place of compassion, honesty, and, most important, loving. Thirty-five years ago, I heard a statement that sums up my approach to communication: "Would you rather be right or loving?" What a concept! I can find my way to loving much more easily and quickly than I can figure out "right." The loving choice when communicating delivers me to peace and freedom more quickly. I love that—and I recommend it.

Through listening to the *sound of God*, I have repeatedly discovered messages that are clear and directional. When I consistently respond to them, the flow of communication becomes natural, useful, authentic, and powerful—a blessing in all ways. What's more, and based on results, I implicitly trust the messages and how to use the information they present in the best possible ways for myself and what's present around me. While this may sound overblown, perhaps this short example will make it clearer.

Early on a Saturday morning around 7:30 a.m., I was driving on a four-lane divided highway with no other cars around. Far ahead, I saw something in the other lane that looked like a cardboard box. I clearly heard that I needed to hit the item with my car and push it to the side of the road. I thought, as anyone would, "What? That's nuts." Doubting that it would work—or work out well for me—I considered ignoring the message and simply driving on. However, that *feeling*—deeper than the gut, deeper than intuition—was present, so I paid attention.

Approaching the item at 70 miles per hour, I could see it was not a box but a small brown sofa. I pictured tapping the sofa so it would angle off to the shoulder of the highway. Inherently trusting this clear message, I went for it, and it worked perfectly. Off the sofa went. Afterward, I pulled over to confirm my car wasn't damaged. Although there hadn't been any other cars on the road all morning, as I stood on the shoulder, an older brown car passed by in the lane where the sofa had been. The car looked almost antique, and the driver was elderly, as was the woman in the passenger seat. Right next to them on this otherwise empty road was another car. *If* I'd ignored the *Sound* and left that sofa in the road, it was clear to me these two cars would have likely collided as the elderly driver swerved to avoid the sofa. I sighed and expressed gratitude as I got into my car and drove on. I even thought that if the sofa's owner came back for it, they could easily retrieve it from the side of the road where it waited, undamaged.

Those moments (and they are a constant in my life) fill me with confidence and gratitude and faith in listening to the *sound of God*. I continue to trust because of the evidence. I continue to take risks, as the outcomes contribute to my *becoming*. As I practice, as I listen, as I trust, as I choose faith, I am embracing risk, claiming the reward—to keep on going. I've added the color of *sacred sound* to my palette as I practice my *art of becoming*.

"Don't be satisfied with stories,
how things have gone with others.
Unfold your own myth."

—RUMI

CHAPTER FIVE

# Affirmations: Making It Real

I liked my alone time. Looking back, I realized that this was a by-product of constantly having doubts about myself. It seemed as if I couldn't get comfortable in any situation no matter how hard I tried. What's more, I devoted a lot of energy to concealing my discomfort (or attempting to). This felt like fear and contraction and looked like shyness—or, in later years, like being overly cautious.

The more these habits persisted, the more difficult it was to find my way out. Affirmations became my antidote. They were the remedy I craved that would ultimately move me out of my limiting beliefs, my doubts, my darkly clouded vision of myself. Affirmations transported me into a new awareness—beyond the filters previously created by my contraction and limitations. For the first time, I became interested in and committed to a more honest and present view of who I was, who I am, and who I continue *becoming*—with practice, of course.

Affirmations added depth to, and gracefully accelerated, my journey of practicing the *art of becoming*.

What is an affirmation?

First, let's look at the dictionary definitions of the noun *affirmation*:

*Oxford English Dictionary*: the action or process of affirming something.

*Collins English Dictionary*: the assertion that something exists or is true.

Affirmations, in the sense I mean them—sometimes called affirmation statements—generally begin with the words *I am*. The intention is to repeatedly affirm something that is true but that may seem beyond reach. Using "I am" statements can help make the quality or behavior become attainable and believable. The statement becomes anchored and secure, ultimately made real to the one speaking, writing, or claiming it. Affirmations have been a powerful form of assistance on my journey, and I have been regularly crafting them for nearly 35 years.

Upon reflection, I came to realize that my harshest, most demeaning, and hurtful statements to myself also began with "I am"—even though I didn't notice it as I said them. For a very long time, I used to say many negative things to myself: "I am stupid, I am ugly, I am bad, I am unlovable, I am lost, I am nothing, I am unworthy, I am hopeless." And, when I did, I was affirming every one of those negative lies.

By the time I learned what affirmations could do, it was difficult for me to find even one positive quality to affirm. I had convinced every part of myself there was nothing good about me. Of course, I did this inwardly, privately, and secretly, while still maintaining a reasonable life and career. I tried not to let on to others, not wanting them to discover the "truth" about me. The best way to keep my secret was to master the art of turning attention toward others in all situations and conversations and rarely share much about myself. I'm sure even people who've known me a long time will learn new things about me by reading this book. I share personal details here—about my life, my process, and keys that assisted me in my discovery of the *art of becoming*—that I never used to openly share, even in close relationships.

As soon as I was starting to become aware of how brokenhearted I was from decades of this negative self-talk—which I believed and adopted as true beyond doubt or debate—I discovered affirmations. I'd begun enrolling in personal growth seminars on personal responsibility and accountability. At one such intensive five-day training, affirmations were introduced as a method of building positive energy and confidence and creating a change in behavior. One evening, we were given a simple exercise to assemble an affirmation based on the following requirements: they must begin with "I am," use action verbs (usually ending in "*-ing*"), and add several positive qualities—including additional language to demonstrate or share these qualities was optional.

With this directive, I could not speak and I certainly could not find a way to complete this exercise. There were about 50 people in the room. It was getting louder and louder as participants were excited to find their words. *I was frozen,* which was probably a good thing, because otherwise I would have run out of the room. By the time the evening ended, I had nothing to show other than tears and horror. The following morning was my last chance, as the remainder of the training built on our affirmations. Almost everyone in the room was well on their way, and I remained in terror.

When time had run out, I had only one thing. One positive thing that I could muster up that was true about me. One thing I could affirm. And I could barely speak it through my tears: "I am alive."

That was my first affirmation. It did not meet all the requirements, but it was accepted, it was enough—enough to start me on my way, even while it took a long time for me to sincerely embrace the truth and power of what saying that did for me.

As I continued practicing with positive statements, I gained greater insight into my history of negative perceptions and self-talk. I came to recognize that the behavior stemmed from my failed, desperate attempts to *understand* everything—people, God, the world, myself, my beliefs, and how I could be myself in the world. When I learned that my very best efforts could not promise understanding, I shifted into *acceptance* instead—accepting people, God, myself, and the world. I became more flexible and more proficient at moving forward with grace along my journey of practicing the *art of becoming*. It was a new beginning! Acceptance is the color of life on my palette as I practice the *art of becoming*.

My use of affirmations has been a tremendous support. It is a key that opened me up to living in the present. It was necessary for me to abandon my old negative "affirmations." And although I practiced fervently until I became very good at stopping them, I still monitor myself for that old habit.

I practice affirmations to anchor my intention to adopt or claim positive qualities as true. I had a moment of awareness when looking from a higher viewpoint and saw *honest* as another benefit when affirming. If I affirm a positive quality, adopt or claim it as true or factual, then it becomes honest within me through affirming. This is a very useful practice and has been essential as I practice the *art of becoming*.

I use several affirmations at any given time, including at least a dozen on my phone that pop up regularly to remind me of good things I'm anchoring in. About 10 years after that first affirmation—and perhaps a hundred successful affirmations later—I participated in an advanced training that included an exercise to craft a new affirmation. I was excited and wanted to make the most of the opportunity. In this supportive and positive environment, I wanted to create a statement that would encompass all I had learned over the past decade. *Freedom* had become the quality that resonated the most with me as my ideal way of being. But I had struggled to work the concept of freedom into an all-encompassing, usable statement—until that training, when I finally got it:

I am free to have it all.

Now that sounded and felt like freedom to me.

The facilitator had to approve our affirmations, and I was a little nervous when I shared mine. Thankfully, this most trusted, admired, and adored warrior teacher sanctioned it for me. He accompanied his approval with a firm caution, reminding me that "having it all" means all: the good, loving, joyful, positive people, places, things, events, feelings, situations, circumstances, *and also* the opposite of each—illness, depression, sadness, hate, negative people, places, and so forth. I understood the meaning and I understood very well what to expect. He and I agreed that I would, and could, manage the entirety of the affirmation.

"I am free to have it all" stemmed from a consciousness of scarcity or lack. This is something I likely inherited from the habits and thinking my parents and grandparents developed during times of scarcity, especially during World War II. Hence, I developed an innate and limiting belief that if I had the basics—a humble income, a safe place to reside, and my health—then it was too much, too selfish, and too rude to have more, and absolutely obscene to want more. In much the same way, it was great to be dedicated and a bright thinker, but it was not okay to demonstrate that outwardly; that was showing off. I had to remain in the background and the shadows.

Affirming the option, the choice, the *freedom* to have it all was extraordinarily risky for me. It exposed me to tremendous judgment and condemnation. At the same time, taking risks—and embracing them wholeheartedly in my actions—was my path to enjoying more expansive behavior in my career and my relationships.

Saying yes to claiming such an expansive opportunity presented a giant leap for me to take. There is no limit to "all." Until then, I'd placed limitations on myself. I could only be "so happy" or "so excited."

Life could only be "so abundant" or so *anything*. For me to be willing to open to more, to have more, to receive more, surely the biggest leap of all was to *become* more.

I hadn't thought much about it in those terms before I took the leap. However, I used the affirmation "I'm free to have it all" for several decades, and I continue to. The statement often shows up, reminding me of the joy I felt the moment I claimed those words. Over the years, I began to believe it was true in a vital and visceral way. I could feel the truth of being free to have it all. And, in that truth, I could see *more* ahead of me, and for me.

Well, time has passed, and I've arrived in that "ahead of me" time now. And I have a newfound recognition that sums up one of the personal rewards of practicing my *art of becoming*. My affirmation has opened up even more profoundly for me. I embrace the greater truth of it. I now affirm this:

I am free to love it all.

The change surprised me. It flowed naturally, as if I had grown into something bigger, more expansive, more mature, and even more free. I am proud of the movement from *have* to *love*. And I can honestly say I find that it's a lot easier to *love* things like sadness or depression or illness than to *have* them!

This updated, upgraded version of my affirmation—after 24 years with the previous version—spilled forward in the course of writing this book. I immediately knew I would include this chapter as one of the powerful lessons that has been integral in my journey.

Risking and practicing have yielded many of my life's wishes, benchmarks, and milestones that amaze and even baffle me: an abundance of compassion and empathy beyond understanding, learning and growing constantly with enthusiasm and wonder, gratitude that rattles my soul and excites my humanity, and a deep peace that exists in me as a tranquil silence even in the most chaotic moments.

Yes, that is what I'm *becoming*—and what I want increasingly to be my foundation as I embrace the expansion, freedom, celebration, and liberation that are my ultimate destinations. The good news is I frequently find fragments of my ultimate destinations along the way, and I recognize and enjoy each one!

In the spring of 2023, I created a new affirmation as I was completing my master's certificate program in advanced spiritual psychology. After decades of practice, this one is the pinnacle of all my attempts to create a statement that is directional and affirms what matters most to me. Visit me at risktobecome.com, and I'll share it with you.

"If you want to fly, you have to give up the things that weigh you down."

—TONI MORRISON

CHAPTER SIX

# Forgiveness: Letting Go

The first real experience that brought forgiveness rushing powerfully into my awareness—in a clear, blatant, and meaningful way—was a day at the grocery store with my mom. I was visiting her as an adult. While approaching the checkout line, I saw a woman I thought I recognized but whom I would never have acknowledged. Rather, if she was who I thought she was—my father's second wife—I'd have ignored and avoided her at all costs. Even though my father was married to her for only five years before his death in 1975, our history was one of judgment and disdain.

Much to my surprise, my mom walked over to her and exchanged casual, caring conversation with a smile while making eye contact. When Mom returned to our cart, I asked if she was speaking to "that woman" and she said "yes." I was shocked, a bit appalled, and even a little angry, asking, "How could you?" I thought my mom was crazy. It turned out she was simply forgiving. My mom did not hold a grudge, did not place blame, did not accuse. She simply was in the moment; she was being true to her kind, caring nature; and she authentically asked the woman about her own well-being and listened to her reply. I witnessed the power of forgiveness in that moment. The freedom in my mom's cadence as she moved and the calm and peace emanating from the tone of her voice contrasted sharply to my own feelings—which were contracted and confused and not peaceful at all. It did not take me long to realize I was the one with a lot to learn that day.

As I found myself discovering the power of forgiveness, I realized I had uncovered the holy grail! Forgiveness became my "go-to" action on the path to *becoming*.

There is great power in taking the risk to forgive. Forgiving inherently includes letting go, which can itself feel risky because it's often hard to give up attachments to our old thinking and behaviors. But the reward far exceeds the risk.

That reward was nothing less than the experience I was longing for, craving, and missing in my life: a visceral sense of greater freedom. A litany of seemingly "unforgivable actions" always pulled me into the past. Upon reflection, I had simply accepted many of those actions—cast upon me by others, by situations, by circumstances. As I forgave and let them go, I was not only finally free from their binds, but I was also surprised that I had permitted them to affect me for so long.

Forgiving literally is *for giving*. And, to me, giving includes gifts. As my forgiving increased, a series of wonderful gifts resulted: more freedom; more happiness; more love; more authentic expression and honesty in my communication, in my relationships, and in my *beingness*. I became happier! I believe this is available to anyone who adopts and practices forgiving and includes it on their journey of *becoming*.

Forgiveness gives me the opportunity to relax and let go of all the spaces where I had to be hypervigilant and was not *free to be*! As I let go of a judgment, an against-ness, or an attachment I had been holding on to (often for reasons that long ago changed, dissolved, or were simply no longer relevant), the resounding truth then becomes clear: Why didn't I make this choice to forgive and let go sooner?

Is forgiving a risk? *Yes.* All the more so when I was

first attempting it, because it was a new behavior and way of being. But with practice, practice, practice, forgiveness became easier. And I came to prefer it to the alternative: holding on to past circumstances and the negative emotions they created while somehow expecting them to produce anything positive for myself or anyone involved.

Is bravery required to forgive? *Yes*. In some cases, quite a lot. Forgiving wasn't a passing thought for me; it was a change in behavior essential to my well-being. I also needed endurance to truly release my patterns of clinging to old stories that were no longer relevant, to stand down when resentment would rear up, and to resist blame and the "right/wrong" dichotomy that limited me.

Is the reward worth it? Is it worth all the work of reviewing and reexamining from a higher altitude; letting go of judgment; getting over the hurdles of anger, resentment, self-righteousness, excuses, self-justification, against-ness, right/wrong thinking;

contending with peer pressure, rivalries, false loyalties to family, church, career, community; wrestling with our own inner fears, doubts, anxieties, illusions, even our "demons"? Absolutely!

Yes! The reward is waiting for you as it was for me. It is worth *all* that if you take the risk. For me, the results are conclusive. The experience of lightness. The freedom. Breathing *in* is suddenly easier. But not only easier—also comforting and nourishing, as there is no obstacle between me and receiving that breath.

The most remarkable thing I learned about choosing forgiveness, I learned very quickly, and I *love* it: forgiving doesn't need the other party's approval, agreement, or comment. And it certainly does not require any degree of reciprocal forgiveness!

The freedom to forgive belongs entirely to me. And it will belong to you as well. Because forgiveness can be completed 100 percent independently of anyone else, it becomes a valuable component of healing.

Forgiveness allows me to let go, regardless of whether another person is or is not present. I can forgive a person (or pet or tree) who is not physically present—whether they are miles away, or imprisoned, or have passed over, or are unconscious, or are unable to respond for any reason. Or I can forgive someone who is nearby, but unable or unwilling to acknowledge it—whether they're not mentally present or their heart is closed off to me, the situation, their world, or themselves. Yes, forgiveness is a holy grail on my path to freedom and liberation.

There is a difference between simply *accepting*—believing I am okay with history and each hurtful incident—and using forgiveness to actually *let go* of these things. When I first recognized this difference, it was like discovering a new dimension—my inner landscape changed to one of expansion and freedom. The change to my self-talk, creative imagination, and belief in myself were worth the risk of embracing forgiveness. I learned to trust in my capability to create my own happiness and joy by letting go and giving up what had been holding me back. Taking the risk to forgive, to let go, illuminated a brilliant and vital path through a dim and murky environment. Where previously my old, incomplete emotions and memories, muddled in judgment and criticism, clouded my inner landscape, now I enjoy the lighter radiance in this renewed perspective. This joy is among the many rewards of adding forgiveness to my palette as I continue practicing my *art of becoming*. Forgiveness is the color of letting go.

Adopting a forgiveness practice has resulted in trackable, almost tangible benefits that have served me outstandingly for a long time. Once I saw the profound and instant shift that true letting go created in my inner life, my behavior quickly changed. There was no going back. And there has been no going back. It's with a whole, joyful heart unencumbered by history that I recommend you become committed to forgiving, too. You could simply begin with just "thinking about it," "checking it out," or "trying it out." I've no doubt you will gradually come to love and commit to the practice, too, because of the value it adds to your quality of life.

I have another hint to offer that has worked well for me, and I promise it works if you allow it to. If I'm unsure if there's anything left to forgive at the end of the day, I take a brief moment before sleep and I simply send my forgiveness to anything that can be forgiven, and I let that be done. No other details required. No questions needed. No deep understanding necessary—although an authentic, heartfelt ask will prove beneficial to the letting go. Ending with *thank you* is not required, but could be the perfect ending to the day for some.

Forgiveness is powerful, so powerful, in fact, that simply setting the intention to let go can start the process in motion. When I am willing to trust in the power of forgiving, I can claim the freedom I desire—the freedom I thrive upon. As I practice the *art of becoming*, I find forgiveness, the holy grail, to be absolutely essential!

"We must let go of the life
we have planned, so as to accept
the one that is waiting for us."

—JOSEPH CAMPBELL

CHAPTER SEVEN

# Ask for Help

Sometimes the most useful action is the most elementary one. The simplest solution can be the best: *Just ask for help.*

This holds true whether we're talking about asking others for assistance or asking in a larger sense. Just ask for help . . . and spiritual assistance may arrive (this has happened to me).

I was historically guilty of *not* asking other people for help. This was learned behavior from a young age. My early attempts at asking for help landed on deaf ears, or maybe it was just easy to ignore little me and my questions. There were limitless reasons why those who might have answered my "asks" (teachers, family, friends, church or community members, etc.) were unavailable to do so. They were consumed by the demands of their busy lives: family, homes, education, thoughts, feelings, and so on. Whatever the case, I learned that asking did not get me help or answers. Often, I simply ended up with more questions.

I was an astute observer by nature. I was a small kid and talked softly. I did not like being loud. It was very easy to overlook me altogether, and if my quiet ask went ignored, I wouldn't make myself known. In all honesty, it became easy for me to stop asking, stand back, stop being a part of things, and observe.

Even so, I wanted to learn. I had questions . . . questions about how I could do things that would be helpful in my environment, and questions that would come to guide my understanding of what was happening around me. It came naturally to me to pose my questions into the silence, the invisible, in my aloneness. And the clear, obvious answers would come—sometimes through the actions all around me or sometimes in a response that I could hear—and which included useful information that actually answered my questions.

I was very young when I became aware of this communication and the flow it provided. It was fun for me to be curious and ask, then pay attention to the response. I consider myself a "solutions-oriented" person, a trait that has proved immeasurably useful in my life. This behavior began in those early years when I was learning on my own.

I learned enough that I began to notice I was learning faster than others around me. I attribute this to asking more useful questions than others may think to ask—albeit all alone and in silence. I also attribute it to the patience I developed by sitting in silence awaiting the answers that would eventually flow to me. Over the years, I've come to trust this method of learning that continues to deepen with experience even today.

I've had a love/hate relationship with patience at times throughout my life. But in practicing the *art of becoming*, patience became easier, more graceful, and more natural for me. As I used everything for my learning, upliftment, growth, expansion, freedom, and liberation, I returned to the patience I had as a small child, sitting and waiting for answers. Giving myself those moments—or sometimes longer—to let the answers come forward always proved worth the wait! My relationship with patience became one of love, joy, and comfort.

This principle added richness to many situations—often when least expected. My intention is to view, and review, situations in a way that lets me use them for my learning. This requires patience and awareness as I observe, act, and complete each experience. One challenging situation where I worked hard to apply these principles was when I had shingles.

As is so often the case with such things, when my shingles appeared, it seemed like the worst possible time for me to be stopped in my tracks. But I realized I had no choice—and that this was a perfect opportunity to practice patience! I learned that shingles usually appear on one side of the body due to nerve pathways. Looking at my face, you could see a clear center line where the virus erupted, covering only half my face from above my eyebrow down to my lips.

So, what did I do? I took a risk I was unaccustomed to and almost immediately asked for help! I called a good friend and help was on the way. It felt like a miracle that, despite everyone's busy schedules, the stars aligned and I was able to see a doctor and get a prescription quickly.

The shingles were scary. They looked frightening, as my face was swollen and the sores were seeping. And they felt scary, causing deep and severe nerve pain and a high fever that exhausted me. Just admitting how much I was suffering was a risk for me—making me exposed and vulnerable. (Upon reflection, I realized embracing the risk of exposure and vulnerability was a good thing.)

I called off work, and the next thing I did was ask myself, "What's this about?" This question helps me uncover and unravel how to use each situation, reveal clues, and grow into greater awareness, which leads to greater freedom in my understanding and outlook. In other words, I will be more prepared for whatever is next when I practice this *usability* principle in each situation.

Finding a way to *use* my shingles episode was a perfect chance to apply this principle. And the experience was one that just kept on giving, since I continued to feel horrible for the next several weeks. As I considered the situation, I recognized, for one thing, what a blessing it was that the shingles were on my face. I live alone,

## ASK FOR HELP

and if the blisters had been on my back or hips, as is more common, it would have been so much more difficult to struggle to care for myself on my own.

Gratitude became a powerful medicine for me. If for no other reason, it helped distract me from feeling wretchedly sick and miserably uncomfortable.

As the pain persisted, I began asking myself what information was missing that might help resolve this. I wondered about the location where the virus first appeared, and since my eye was the starting point of the first blister, I asked, "Is there something I'm not seeing?" I looked inward more acutely and honestly than I had allowed myself to do for a long time, as I'd been distracted by the busyness of my work and my outer world.

After a week, the nerve pain worsened, traveling from my right eye over my head to the back of my neck and back again to my right ear. It was excruciating, and it was clear this pain wouldn't stop until I asked, "What am I not feeling?" The endurance required in asking to discover this felt very risky for me. I was uncertain, and feared the physical and emotional outcomes and where they might lead. Asking this question was especially crucial as I am a distinctly kinesthetic feeling person. "What am I not feeling?" I knew asking this question was essential as it would lead to my relief. I had to endure the pain while waiting and listening for the response.

I focused on these questions, and answers surfaced. I listened for the information and recognized the *usability*. Additionally, I let go of what was not usable. I had no new questions. I began to feel better and returned to work with a renewed outlook amplified by the gratitude that accompanied the illness.

What is interesting is that, although I processed the help that came forward at the time, I no longer have any idea what the information was. I do know it was deeply emotional, profound for me to acknowledge, and very useful. I claimed the truth in the moment, and then I let it go. I used the information and the letting go to move me forward into greater freedom, releasing what I no longer needed.

*Usability* and *using* are important keys in the process of *becoming*. I was practicing intensely in those weeks, aware of what was present, wanting to understand, and asking for help. I am adding a combination of compatible colors to my palette here: the colors of "asking" and "using." They add dimension to my palette in much the same way they add dimension to my awareness.

It's worth noting that I asked for help in two ways, both important: practical help from my friend, and inwardly, where the greater truth is always waiting when I am ready to access it. I experience the latter as tapping into Source, the All, Inner Wisdom. This silent asking *will* deliver a response. Observe vigilantly as an answer may show up where you least expect it.

I believe I had a greater prayer and asked for help

before the shingles erupted. The help showed up in the form of shingles, allowing me the pause and the purpose to look deeper, ask deeper, and receive deeper. I got the help I was seeking partly because I allowed myself to use what was present as my answer rather than waiting for what I thought the answer may be or how it would be delivered.

Help led to more understanding. It assisted me with moving forward into freedom—into more authentic and honest seeing, feeling, and thinking. I use this practice more often than not, even with routine everyday events. *Becoming* can happen all the time—with both big and small movements.

I sometimes ask myself, "What am I *becoming*?" I don't have a clear answer yet. I suspect that's because I'm looking for something intricate and complex when the answer most likely is simple. We'll see. I do know that as I ask for help, receive answers, and use the information, I am consistently growing. I am more present with myself and others, and more available for new experiences beyond prior conditions. This allows for more joy and authenticity in my relationship with myself, with others, and with situations.

There is one more step with asking for help, which is to integrate the answer the moment it becomes clear. Otherwise, the lag between the moment of recognizing clear, usable information and accepting it can create havoc. Havoc comes from filling that gap with "what if," "but I could have/should have," "I wish I had," or "I didn't because." That *because* is a trap. Put bluntly, it's an excuse. The habit of pausing to make the shift from awareness into excuses is 100 percent unnecessary. It involves looking back, a delay from the here and now, pulling me away from the *gift* of awareness in the present. Awareness moves us forward and upward and inward and outward into *being* truer to our authentic divine nature, the one we are *becoming* from our first breath to our last. Take a risk the moment you know it is the right thing to do. Override the pause that gives havoc a way in. Skip excuses all the time in all ways. The benefits will be palpable!

"Your vision will become clear only when you look into your own heart. Who looks outside, dreams; who looks inside, awakens."

—CARL JUNG

CHAPTER EIGHT

# Integrity Amplified

It seems as though I was always observing. My earliest memory of doing so was upon first arriving home from the hospital. I observed the room where I was lying on the table, the light shining through the window, my mother standing over me, my brother standing next to her trying to see "the baby." I also felt their uneasy emotions as they spoke to one another. I could not know that much of what I was seeing and feeling, though very real, had nothing to do with me. I was absorbing images, words, and emotions from others when I was too young to understand the difference between *me* and *them*. It took a lot of maturing, a lot of learning, and a lot of time to sort that out in my later years. But as I was practicing the *art of becoming*, I knew I wanted to become just *me*, free of anything that is not mine.

Observation came naturally to me, always accompanied by an array of details. This was my "wide-eyed" approach—taking in and recording a multitude of detailed information I was seeing and sensing. This was compounded by the empathic nature I was blessed with, which registered a multitude of detailed feelings. Complex is a fair description of what I was experiencing.

And so, *complexity* became my natural approach. This meant drawing on the details—of my experiences, vast observations, and sensitive feelings—and then applying them to each new opportunity, task, situation, or job that presented itself to me. Using this approach, I was able to quickly assess a new opportunity and creatively visualize a path to results. This method has been a great resource for me. It has helped me say yes to taking risks, to trying new things, and to navigating new opportunities. I trust this practice as authentic and honest because it's based on actual experience.

I trusted this practice and method of learning as authentic and honest because it was based upon my direct experience. I then recognized authenticity and honesty as fundamental qualities of my integrity.

Paraphrasing from *Merriam-Webster's* dictionary: integrity is *the quality of being honest; the state of being whole*. I assigned integrity as my compass or barometer for my behavior. This stemmed from both my early lessons about being "good" and what I learned by observing behavior that varied from less honest to completely dishonest. Watching situations in which people behaved outside of integrity, and the consequences that followed—often cruel, painful, corrupt, and devastating to others—stuck with me. Acting with honesty and integrity became a commitment at the forefront of my awareness.

Over time, this habit of complexity morphed into a practice I designed to keep me "safe." A series of unexpected life events that were sudden, tragic, scary, and often deeply hurtful turned my attention toward insecurity. I began to contract. I felt compelled to be more structured in my inward thoughts and processes—as if I could control what happened around me and even to *me*! That was a misidentification for sure. Still, I did my best.

The attempt to connect my safety to my integrity led me to pause, whereas before I had been more *instant* in my astute awareness and thoughtful understanding. This new *pause* behavior felt aligned with integrity to me—while it also took my *complex* approach and complicated it one step further. In those pauses, I began to over-anticipate, over-plan and over-evaluate. Basically, I over-complicated new situations and new opportunities. It is only in hindsight (and "high sight," as in altitude) that I am able to identify this behavior more honestly—and with more authentic integrity.

Interestingly, my contracting and pausing did not limit my taking risks. I continued to reach for each new opportunity, to learn and grow and expand into my goal of freedom, trusting myself through the hesitation before making each new decision. I kept going in this way even though I slowly began to notice unnecessary challenges that accompanied the more complex behavior. I eventually came to recognize that I could drop *complexity* altogether. *Simplicity* ultimately became my preference.

Simplicity was a good approach for me and a good partner for my commitment to integrity. I discovered *simplicity* when I slowed down or even stopped briefly, and the scared part of me got quiet. I noticed a stark difference. I quickly knew I wanted more of this different way of being. This approach was worth practicing, and I wanted *simplicity* to be an aspect of who I am becoming! *Simplicity* is a new color on the palette of my *art of becoming*!

Also, I eventually realized that my habit of *complexity* kept me busier than I needed to be. It kept me questioning beyond a reasonable doubt. And, in all honesty, it kept me too occupied, keeping me from being in the present moment. It did this by overstimulating me with more details than were necessary for me to exist within my desired commitment to integrity. For a very long time I was not aware of this pattern. I didn't recognize the busyness was distracting me from my authentic beingness. It was distracting me from *becoming*. Wow!

Learning this lesson is among the top 10 discoveries to which I attribute my current joy, experience of freedom, and sense of being.

This discovery was *mind-blowing*. For me, freedom lies

in the heart and soul. For something to be mind-blowing is a welcome comfort and pleasure, a giant win! I experience integrity as a quality that surpasses the mind—for me, it is a way of being.

It's worth noting that it's probably best to have one's mind blown when there is an alternative in view. In my case that was claiming my *art of becoming* and actively embracing my *authentic being,* my*self.* Being takes practice, takes commitment, takes intention, and employs integrity. Choosing into authentically being is hard and risky—partly because it can be unfamiliar, uncomfortable, even unknown in the beginning— yet it is worth every moment of the effort. On the way, I discovered this: Being is authentic. Being happens in the present. Being is less complicated. Being is now. Being is honest. Being is freedom. Being simply is.

I am now even more invested in my pursuit of the integrity that pulls me toward my divine *becoming*. At the core of my integrity is my *beingness*. To reiterate this paraphrase of *Merriam-Webster's* definition, which sums up my understanding of the reasons to choose and embrace integrity—*integrity is the quality of being honest; the state of being whole*.

In my earlier attempts to be "honest and whole"—alongside my astute observation and deep emotional sensitivity—there were many areas that seemed to overlap. It was not until I embraced the concept of altitude (taking a second look or a "new sight" from high above) that I could begin to see that the overlap was not real. There was in fact space between the feelings I was experiencing. And that space showed me the more honest truth that sometimes, although I was sensitively aware of them, it evidenced that many of those feelings were not *mine*.

There is openness, freedom, joy, ease, and grace present when I experience alignment with integrity—my *quality of being honest; the state of being whole*. However, much to my surprise, that is not a given just because I want it to be eternally present.

It is up to me to repeatedly align with integrity—to consistently think in alignment, to feel in alignment, to choose in alignment, to behave and act in alignment, to walk and breathe in alignment—so I then can *be* and become aligned. It's a practice, and sometimes it is an uncomfortable choice to remain aligned. I want to make that uncomfortable choice without hesitation and beyond doubt or resistance or uncertainty. That is what directed me to expand, increase, to make it bigger and louder, to amplify! How could I do that?

What if I applied impeccability to my practice of integrity? That would clearly amplify choosing and aligning with integrity *"in accordance with the highest standards of propriety."*

This comes from the *Oxford English Dictionary*:

> *impeccable* (adjective): (of behavior, performance, or appearance) in accordance with the highest standards of propriety.

I remember the first time I witnessed someone truly exhibit impeccability. It was a profound observation and created a lasting impact and a visceral feeling that I would reference going forward. This person instantly took command of a large, unruly crowd by communicating with authority—not harsh, not threatening, simply true! He was clear, present, confident, and in his authentic *beingness*. I was in awe. As I watched, *impeccable* was the word that resounded in me and around me. It was astonishing! In that moment, I said a prayer to work at his side one day so I could learn more about this quality of impeccability directly. My prayer was answered a decade later and it was a good prayer, worth the wait, and worth the learning!

I have been very fortunate to know and work closely with industry leaders who demonstrated leadership with impeccability. I have great admiration and respect for them. Also, I learned valuable leadership skills while working with them. I came to recognize the risks it takes to make hard choices while skillfully employing impeccability.

Based on what I witnessed and learned, I recognized the next step for me in my path to *becoming*—and in my commitment to myself—was to implement *impeccable integrity*.

As I amplify my intention in this way, I feel more aligned, the strength to stay aligned, and happy to have arrived at this expansion into my *art of becoming*. I am adding the amplified, resounding color of *impeccability* to my palette.

"You may not control all the events that happen to you, but you can decide not to be reduced by them."

—MAYA ANGELOU

CHAPTER NINE

# Perception: Take a Second Look

I had a memorable experience that continually reminds me of the importance of *perception*. What I see—and the story I tell myself about it—is always worth a second look before I draw any conclusions! This experience remains a creative life lesson, encouraging me to take the risk of remaining open to interpretation and *re-interpretation* of first impressions.

Early one morning, I was taking in the scenery as I drove to a new work location. I was driving through a storm that is typical of winter in Southern California. I was not too far from the ocean, which increased the intensity of the pouring rain and forceful winds.

I turned onto a new street that was lined with cypress trees—elegant, tall, narrow evergreens that grow to a point and gracefully reach straight up to the heavens, reminding me of angels. These particular trees, however, leaned far toward the east. The heavy winds and relentless rain of the storms bent the trees further and further with each gust. It looked so harsh to me. They no longer were able to stand tall and elegant.

I felt sad for these unhappy and unfortunate trees who surrendered to the repeated thrashings of the storms. It was clear they were losing the battle against so many winters of wind and were no longer able to stand tall. They would not gracefully reach up to the heavens ever again. The poor, sad trees.

I didn't think about the cypress trees again until my drive to work the following day. These poor, crooked trees were taking another beating on this stormy, wintry day!

On the third day, I was happy to notice the sun had returned. It was a beautiful morning, with the perfectly clear blue skies that come after the rain. As I turned the corner to drive up the street with the cypress trees, I was astonished. I could not help but smile ear to ear! These beautiful trees were as graceful as any. In the glistening golden warmth, each of the trees purposefully reached *toward* the sun. Yes, they bent eastward, but that was because their silhouettes arched in the direction of the morning light. The trees had made their choice. They knew what they wanted—the glorious sun—and they were going to go for it, reach for it, and their unconventional shape was a result of them pursuing their happiness. They leaned eastward because that's what made them happy. And that day, I saw that the cypress trees were extraordinarily happy!

I laughed, recognizing these cypresses most likely were unaffected by the harsh conditions of the winter storms. That's *just winter* for them, and they bend with ease. Another interesting fact, now that I thought about it: they did not resist the wind; they simply moved with it and patiently surrendered, awaiting the day the sun would shine again! They took the risk to give up "standing tall" to have what they wanted instead. Upon first impression, it may seem like they had lost the battle to the storm, but, in fact, they won the war, their war to reach for the sun.

What a lovely lesson, and how useful it has been to me many times over. I find special joy in the things nature teaches me. And I am deeply grateful.

So, that is my story of *perception*. Had I never driven up that street on a sunny morning, I may never have recognized the greater truth that a second look evidenced. As I practice my *art of becoming*, I'm adding the color called *perception* to my palette.

I would like to think that I, too, may be known by more than a first impression whenever possible. Each of us deserves a second look, a reinterpretation, and even more than that, to be known authentically. I like practicing that!

"True happiness is not found in
what we achieve
but in who we become
through love and connection."

—ARTHUR BROOKS

CHAPTER TEN

# Listen with Your Heart

From the start, I was immediately interested in everything. Wide-eyed and sensitive, my focus was outward and my reality was the outer world—what was happening to people around me and what was happening to people in other places. I observed everything I could access: my home and family; my neighborhood; my schools and the students, teachers, and staff there; the TV and radio news and programs; newspapers and magazines; our treasured encyclopedias; the sky; and more. It was a lot of information to process!

This changed drastically when I learned of another way of being. I began to consider and investigate my inner world. That was the real turning point where my practice toward the *art of becoming* began. It was my first recognition that I had the power to stop absorbing my outer world, my outer sense of reality, and the multitude of outer experiences I both observed and participated in.

In order to fully embrace this new approach of connecting to my inner awareness, I discovered it was necessary to look back—to reexamine the past and become acquainted with this inner part of myself that, though long neglected, had been there all along!

Over many decades, this process of engaging my inner awareness has evolved and unfolded, requiring dedicated attention and intention. I was all in to learn about that inner world that had eluded me for so long. Risk was certainly involved: How could I find time to do this work, given my career commitments? How could I pay for the education I desired and needed? What was I about to uncover? Could it all backfire and reveal my worst fears—that the negative messages I absorbed about myself from the outer world might be true?

Interestingly, it never occurred to me that what could be revealed was the greatest blessing of acceptance, connection, compassion, freedom, joy, and an unconditional loving that surpasses understanding.

If this process was going to work, it was essential that I go back, look back, and learn about my inner awareness starting from my earliest memories, then working forward through my life's timeline. This process took a long time, involving all kinds of classes, research, achievements, degrees, plus deep personal unconditional review and learning. Altogether, I logged over 10,000 classroom hours across four decades (I like to be thorough).

I made a lifetime commitment to continue the process every day using the keys and tools I'm writing about in this book (along with quite a few others). I practice all the time! Every day, every place, every situation becomes a classroom steeped with opportunity for learning. The journey is always in motion, always moving into greater awareness on the path to *becoming*.

I discovered that a deeper, greater peace and freedom became available in the present after resolving a whole lot of history. When I looked back as an exercise, using the viewpoint of altitude—observing from above—to reveal and see more of the genuine landscape of events, things finally made much more sense. With this greater view, I was able to *see* events big and small with clarity, honesty, and simplicity—including many adjacent factors unknown to me in real time. I could experience compassion, acceptance, and understanding thanks to that new clearer view. I was able to let confusion, anger, judgment, and control (or lack thereof) dissolve and slip away.

This new viewpoint allowed for unconditional acceptance and opened the doors to forgiveness. Walking through those doors was a choice, and an important one necessary to the peace and freedom I was seeking. Accepting the risk of choosing forgiveness is my holy grail as I practice my *art of becoming*.

From this new perspective, deeper understanding and healing were available. As I allowed and accepted what was available, I experienced a graceful entry point into unconditional loving regardless of the memory of events. I chose grace, and in so doing, moved forward in my journey of *becoming*. I made a commitment to practice this regularly. Grace is a gorgeous and effervescent color I'm adding to my palette.

This change—this upgrade, adjustment, modification to my way of being in this new and comforting stillness of peace and freedom—definitely influenced my ability to listen. This is when I recognized the value of sound and the sacredness of my listening.

I knew it would be valuable to match what I was listening to with what aligned with (and was in service to) my inner environment. That inner environment includes my heart and soul, where my most intimate and profound sense of peace resides. That is why listening with my heart was essential—where the sacred sound is impeccably honest and trustworthy. I learned to be very attentive to what I was listening to. And part of that *what* includes: Who am I listening to? Where is the sound coming from? Is the sound serving my journey toward *becoming*?

I often experienced that Sacred Sound as I practiced listening with my heart. And as I practiced this as part of my *art*, I was able to hear the sound of my *becoming*. It was in perfect pitch and rhythm with my breath, my heartbeat, the movement of life through me. I could hear my oneness with both the *all* around me and the *nothingness* beyond me. I liked that, and with practice, it became easier, more natural, and almost involuntary. I'm adding *listening with my heart* as a radiant, glittery color in my palette as I practice my *art of becoming*.

Much to my surprise and delight, it quickly became clear to me when I slipped out of that comfort. I could feel the change in rhythm and my breath. And that became an extremely useful key for me in both inner *and* outer awareness. I continue to learn and practice minimizing the length of time between realizing I've slipped out of rhythm and returning to the comforting stillness of peace and freedom.

Did you ever notice *heart* has the word *hear* in it? Hint, hint, *hint*!

LISTEN WITH YOUR HEART!

How interesting is that?

That was a little comedic to me. An exercise in *what I see*. I write those words laughing about the *art of becoming*, because the word *art* also appears in the word *heart*! So much to see, consider, use, and learn, even in the simplicity of just five letters assembled and reassembled.

"It's not how much we give
but how much love
we put into giving."

—MOTHER TERESA

CHAPTER ELEVEN

# Philanthropy Unlimited

My mother embodied a generous spirit. Most often this would present itself as an act of helping others. She was simply a natural when presented with an opportunity to help. She would find a way—the time, the resources—and it was always done with joy and loving care. And, more important, she always offered help selflessly, expecting nothing in return. That seems almost counterintuitive when I think of the moderate financial circumstances she managed under, as a single mother of seven children working in a factory for a wage that seemed sinful in our America.

I spent a lot of time with my mother growing up. She was good at a lot of things that made her good at helping in a lot of ways and in a lot of places. Her authentic smile was truly radiant, warm, and contagious. She always wore lipstick when she left the house (not out of any particular vanity, but simply because lipstick was popular when she was a young woman working in Rochester, New York, during the war) and, consequently, her smile was beautiful and inviting, just like her warm heart. I began wearing pink lipstick at age fifteen—the moment she permitted me to leave the house wearing it. I loved it! I loved the way it looked, how it felt, and that it reminded me of her. Eventually my colors became shades of red like the ones my mom wore in her youth.

She talked to strangers all the time, always with a

smile, and her natural way of being would elicit a welcome response. In all my years of observing, I cannot recall anyone ever responding harshly to her, and I found that surprising and inspiring. As I was more of a quiet observer in those early years, it took me a while to adopt the open and kind behavior I learned from her. It was risky for me, as I was fearful that others would reject or dismiss me (a throwback to my early childhood when that was my experience). I was happily surprised by the result! It was fun and felt good to interact with strangers in random public places like on the bus that I took to work daily or in the grocery store—so many opportunities! The surprise of my interaction would prompt others' spontaneous warm reciprocation—and I enjoyed that the most. A new friendship would instantly form and last only as long as the ride to the next bus stop or the time it took to move along the line to the cash register. These brief and real interactions were well worth the risk as they were filled with *loving for humankind*!

*Philanthropy* is derived from the Greek words *philos*,

which means "loving," and *anthropos*, which means "humankind." Thus, *philanthropy* can be roughly defined as *love for humankind*. That is the broad perspective—one that absolutely matters to me. This is definitely the deep, vibrant color of *love of humanity* on my palette as I practice my *art of becoming*!

Here are the dictionary definitions of the noun *philanthropy*:

> *Oxford English Dictionary*: the desire to promote the welfare of others, expressed especially by the generous donation of money to good causes.

> *Merriam-Webster:* goodwill to fellow members of the human race; *especially:* active effort to promote human welfare.

I have long enjoyed participating in volunteering, service, joining groups in helpful efforts, and pitching in as often as possible. I've been involved in global giving, foundation giving, and personal giving for as long as I can remember. I would regularly give money, time, and a broad variety of resources available to me.

But there was one day in 1997 when a moment of unconditional, authentic *love for humankind* altered my experience. I recognized a deeper quality, clarity, and experience of true philanthropy. I saw what my commitment would be going forward, and I designed what I would come to think of as my *giving compass* to guide my way.

I was a brand-new resident of Ojai, California, making my first trip to the local laundromat. Ojai is a small, sweet, and very warm town. With its beautiful world-class resort and spa, it's also somewhat of a tourist attraction. This laundromat was not on the main street, but tucked away a few streets back. When I drove up and parked my car, I noticed mostly migrant workers there, both women and men, with their children. It was a busy time in Ojai with seasonal workers in town harvesting citrus, avocados, olives, figs, and other crops.

I finished my laundry and was loading my car when a man approached me. He was tall and slender and clearly had already put in a hard day's work. His skin was dark and showed signs of many days in the sun even though he wore a wide-brimmed straw hat for protection. He looked at me with the most honest eyes I've ever seen. And those eyes helped him communicate, as it was quickly evident that he did not speak any English—and he was correct to assume I did not speak his language, either. I was so absorbed in this solely visual exchange that I'm not sure what else he did to try to wordlessly communicate, but as his children looked on from nearby, I think he opened his hand, which had a quarter in it. The message was that he was in need of another quarter for the machines to help him finish his laundry. I had lots of coins and was happy to give them to him. This man stood still in palpable humility that was like a magnet, pulling me to keep standing there before him. He then reached out and gave me the most perfect orange. Both his eyes and mine welled with tears.

There was an exchange of recognition. He shared with me the fruits of his labor that day. And he offered this in exchange with the most heartfelt, heart-*full*, authentic gratitude. I could also feel from him the times he had been denied and even judged in other such incidents when other people may have turned away. And it brought to the surface the times I had been denied and judged and rejected. We saw one another at our deepest, purest nature of *human kindness*. We never uttered a sound. In complete silence, we nodded, and we parted.

It was tough for me to decide to eat the orange. I wanted to keep it and remember. But I knew that would not have made the man happy. He wanted to share what mattered to him. I ate the orange. I remember it tasted heaven-sent, because it was. Such an exchange was a perfect moment of giving spontaneously and unconditionally; helping and exchanging honestly. It was authentic *love for humankind*. Each time I recall this memory of the man who touched my heart and soul in the ordinariness of an Ojai laundromat, it serves as a teaching moment.

I recognized that the tall, kind father was expressing his philanthropy in his way. And I am grateful I had the wit and the presence to be with him—to partake and be present in the gifted moment of exchanging personal authenticity. Also, I knew this lesson would stay with me and influence my own philanthropy. I would come to embrace the ways the simplest acts of giving can have profound results. That day, the results were mine, just as I was the recipient of the riches of his philanthropy!

I felt the power of looking into another's eyes, honoring all they are in that moment. What a remarkable thing it is to truly connect with a mutual compassion that surpasses our unique circumstances—culture, history, gender, language. In that moment, we were the same: human beings, each with a heart and soul, each respecting the other with compassion and gratitude.

I knew my *giving compass* would not be bound by dollars and cents. While my compass includes financial giving that, of necessity, often does not include personal interaction, I also provide professional services free of charge and volunteer in many ways. On those occasions I genuinely share *love for humankind*, enjoying the exchanges with each person involved. And serving in person is not only about giving—I also receive deeply and experience a special hope and encouragement when I engage in philanthropy in this special way.

Had I never taken the risk to engage with the stranger who approached me—choosing trust over fear, haste, or the ignorance of disinterest—I would not have learned of my true north, the impact of sharing love for humankind, and the value of my *giving compass*. My compass is also heavily focused on simply seeing others: looking into a stranger's eyes when saying hello, remaining present with others when speaking kind words. Acts of my everyday communication include listening sensitively, speaking tenderly, and writing lovingly in cards and notes. Other forms of interaction might be a gentle touch of understanding or encouragement, giving something of my own away when the moment lends itself to a joyful recipient, acts of kindness—some random, some intentional, some spontaneous, some selfish (meaning the times where I feel as though I'm actually the one getting the greatest joy).

You, too, may have a list of ways you give in the name of *love for humankind*. What I have found to be the most important is taking the moment to engage and be present. Looking into the other person's eyes both amplifies and grounds this exchange, as it is a demonstration of respect and compassion, just as the migrant worker showed me. The experience was a life lesson I am grateful to claim and use as I journey on my path to *becoming*.

My *giving compass* is expansive, and the choices are many. Its true north forever points to *love for humankind*. I'm adding the color of philanthropy to my palette—it grounds my art in riches.

One little comment—something I learned during the COVID pandemic when masks were mandatory and there was a lot of isolation. I was living in a temporary first-floor apartment. I'd occasionally see the neighbor who lived above me in passing and we'd engage briefly from behind our masks. As I moved out two months later, I saw my neighbor, and in her happiest, warmest voice she said goodbye and added, "I'll never forget your smile." I loved that. It was evidence to me of all I had learned from my mother and from that tall, silent migrant worker—because I wore my mask every time I left the apartment. My neighbor will "never forget" my smiling eyes.

This was exciting to me. It was evidence that the decades of practicing my *art of becoming* was working. And it left me feeling joyful, with deep gratitude and hopeful anticipation to keep going! I am happy.

"You have treasures hidden within you—extraordinary treasures—and bringing them out takes work and faith and focus and courage."

—ELIZABETH GILBERT

CONCLUSION

# Knowledge, Gratitude, and Destination

I remember how valuable it has been for me to acknowledge, embrace, and claim out loud that I am a student of life. That statement made sense to me. It offered credibility to my unique lifestyle of risk, encompassing several decades of bold, courageous, and often seemingly unconventional choices. It also serves as a solid reply when I'm asked why I chose to live a life outside the traditional examples around me.

As an aspiring student of life—with a judicious intention to "graduate" someday—I also began to recognize the important implication that I am the one responsible for my experience of this life. I'm responsible for how I think or feel about my life, I'm responsible for how I think or feel about others, I'm responsible for how I treat myself, and I'm responsible for how I treat others. I'm also responsible for how I think or feel in response to how others treat me—or treat each other or the planet or anything else. Attending to these responsibilities is a priority and directs my journey of practicing the *art of becoming*. I have decided to name the palette holding all my colors *responsibility*. Responsibility gloriously anchors my purpose for practicing the *art of becoming* just as it anchors the multitude of colors I've not only discovered thus far, but also those yet to be defined, claimed, revealed.

Have you heard the saying "to whom much is given, much is expected"? I was given a strong heart. With that, I am aware it warranted a broad and varied landscape of experience and opportunity to learn and grow toward *becoming*. I was also given a nature that commits to what matters to me (with a side of stubborn). This has served me well in the long run—my commitment (and stubbornness) are what allowed persistent practicing to come naturally to me.

Art has endless qualities. Here are a few of my personal favorites: mystery, beauty, diversity, science, fantasy, illusion, reality, color, illumination, emotion, silence, spirituality. With all that in mind, I discovered that practicing *becoming* as an *art* is simply (lusciously, delectably) expansive. It holds plenty of options and outlets to use in the process that leads to my *becoming*. I only have to risk yet again each time I encounter limitations, resistance, fear, and doubt. I'm learning with each risk that those negatives are illusions and will quickly dissolve when confronted with honesty, with *love of humankind*, and with action.

Mastery is a decision. It is a commitment that has no end. Mastering the art of becoming is a journey. My journey. My art. And I believe that journey can be whatever I want it to be. I use all that I have been given and all that I am learning. In much the same way, it can be whatever the artist wants it to be, and whatever the artist wants to *become* is completely a unique and personal choice. Only the artist will know their unique path and art. That is the epitome of the "to whom much is given" process: we each are given our unique life to design and work with.

On my journey of *becoming*, I have learned to anticipate not only the destination, but also all that is necessary to achieve it. I was shown early on that my most abundant gifts were in the areas of awareness, observation, and learning. And my bonus gift is that I was given the promise of endurance *to the end*. I am deeply grateful for each quality and for so much more.

Gratitude is the color I am adding to my palette

just now. It is a multidimensional, expansive color that shines brightly and always will, regardless of situation, environment, or circumstance.

In this, my first book, I've shared just a few of the guiding tools, keys, or methods of practice that supported my journey of risking into greater freedom. I do my best every day. Some days are better than others. Have I ever had a 100 percent day using one, or all, of these techniques in my practicing? I doubt it. And I'm pretty sure I'd remember that day—or some part of it—if it occurred! Does that fact interfere with my passion and commitment to move in the direction of *becoming* with practice every day? Absolutely not. I am practicing toward my own version of Vivaldi's *Four Seasons*, Handel's *Messiah*, Philip Glass's *Koyaanisqatsi*, John Lennon's *Imagine*. I am practicing toward my masterpiece.

One day, when I was a kid, it was me and the neighborhood boys plus my younger brothers excitedly choosing our superpowers. As you can imagine, the boys chose being invisible, flying, and X-ray vision. I chose knowledge! It just made the most sense to me. Not in a know-it-all way, but as an opportunity to learn more usable information about everywhere and everything. I have a feeling *The Wizard of Oz* left quite an impression on me—the all-knowing wizard was just a regular guy! Anyone could know things! Asking and praying for knowledge as a superpower remains with me to this day. It's my responsibility to make it real as I practice my *art of becoming*.

To accomplish that dream, I must keep going, continue risking, continue learning, continue becoming more. I am becoming more authentic and truer to what matters to my heart and soul. They are the drivers in this journey and, on a good day, I'm not only comfortably along for the ride—I'm loving the ride.

Can I see the destination? Sometimes I have the tiniest glimpse. And that alone is powerful enough to keep my attention, my commitment, my passion, my fortitude and stamina, my prayers and wishes, all singularly focused and moving in that direction.

Do you have a direction? A destination? Will you take a risk? Are you on your way to practicing the *art of becoming* with intention, tools, keys, and passion?

I'd love to keep the conversation going with you, as we each practice our *art of becoming*. You can find me at risktobecome.com.

"There is no excess in the world so commendable as excessive gratitude"

—Jean de la Bruyere

# Acknowledgments

I am so pleased to pay tribute and acknowledgment to these wonderful people:

My Wayshowers with deepest heartfelt gratitude for their unwavering commitment to the blessings of the power of Living Loving. You are my True North. My heart is yours. Thank You.

My Teachers, Educators, Facilitators who enhanced my journey of self-discovery. Friends, Family,

Employers, Clients, Co-workers, Neighbors, Communities both professional and spiritual, and everyone whose paths I've crossed on all levels. Each of you has been a teacher, a role model, a classmate, an example, a hero, a helper, a prophet, an expert, and a unique contributor toward my process of becoming. You demonstrated your own authenticity, wisdom, vulnerability, strength, loving, and radiance as I observed, learned, and then applied to my own process of learning and growing. Thank you.

The beauty and abundance of this Planet, which teaches me so much about life cycles, about giving and receiving, about the graceful honesty of nature and the perspective I gain from observing the strength and forgiving resilience of God's creation. Thank you.

An added and extra special acknowledgment and Thank You to:

My publisher, the Collective Book Studio—Angela

and Elisabeth who quickly said "YES" and guided my journey with their brilliant enthusiasm; beloved Bridget who is an angel without wings and was a blessing beyond words with every word; and the entire creative production team.

My Soul Sister Katie Riess who has been my rock! She walked at my side every step of the way with unbridled joy, kindness, the perfect blend of patience with encouragement to keep me on deadline, and unconditional unwavering support in all ways. Plus a special thanks for so much fun, laughter, tears, honesty, transparency, family, and absolute joy along the way—so much more is yet to come! Thank you also to KT Media Strategies for sharing her with me so generously.

Whether one refers to Source, Energy, The Universe, The One, Master Consciousness, Guru, etc.—I call it God and acknowledge such a presence in every word. Thank you.

# About the Author

Patty Elvey is a dedicated student of life using every experience for learning and greater awareness. Her 40+ years working with thought leaders and corporate visionaries spanning the industries of legal tech, quantum AI, media, and healthcare provides the foundation for her work uniting clients' professional goals with their personal passions. Patty's uniquely holistic approach uncovers strengths and builds a road map for achieving their unrealized dreams. In her debut book, *Practicing the Art of Becoming*, Patty shares personal insights that inspired and ignited her journey of becoming. A longtime resident of Menlo Park, California, Patty now enjoys splitting her time between the East and West Coasts.

Find out more at www.risktobecome.com.